THESIS WRITER'S GUIDE

MAKING AN ARGUMENT IN THE HUMANITIES AND SOCIAL SCIENCES

MICHAEL E. CHAPMAN

Trebarwyth Press

Reading, Massachusetts

Publishing and Printing
Published 2010 by Trebarwyth Press
15 High Street, Reading, MA 01867
Typeset in Adobe Garamond Pro
Printed and bound in the People's Republic of China by the
Beijing Huiyuanruncai Printing Company
Acid-free paper
15 14 13 12 11 10   1 2 3 4 5
Library of Congress Control Number: 2010932817
ISBN-13:   978-0-9786597-3-8
ISBN-10:   0-9786597-3-2

CONTENTS

INTRODUCTION

If you intend to produce a high-quality, groundbreaking senior research paper, graduation thesis, MA thesis, PhD dissertation, or journal article, whether in English, Chinese, or any other language, and in conformity with internationally-recognized standards, then this guide is for you. My perspective happens to be that of a historian, so naturally I will draw examples from my experience of doing history rather than, say, philosophy. Yet the system I describe applies just as well to related disciplines like ethnography, international relations, or literary studies, as well as to most social sciences fields from political science to sociology that may use alternative styles of citation. While I was born in Britain in 1954, I trained most recently in the United States during 2002–6; I mention this because since the 1990s American historiography has improved on the European model characterized by multi-sentence quotations, passive voice, and understated argumentation to create expositions that are more textually immersive, actor driven, and argumentative. As distinct from the British English taught in European, Indian, and Asian schools, American English furthermore offers benefits of flow and precision, and is now normative at leading journals and publishing houses worldwide.

Colleagues in China urged me to publish this guide from a concern that Asian theses had become repositories of information rather than interpretive analyses. Indeed, at a recent graduate seminar at Peking University's history department, I asked my PhD students, "What is a thesis?" to which one replied, "My topic," and another added, "My research." They were surprised to hear the standard dictionary definition: "A thesis is *a proposition advanced as an argument*." Yes, a thesis is about a topic, and, for sure, it does present research, but it interprets that research as evidence to build a case. Thesis writers are the scholarly equivalent of trial lawyers. To put it another way, a thesis, dissertation, or journal article that does not make an argument is unworthy of a degree or publication.

For ease of use, as well as readability by non-native English speakers, I have divided the process of brainstorming, researching, writing, and publishing a thesis into four chapters, each of which I subdivide into tasks, and subdivide again virtually at the paragraph level into important points I wish to make. All this dividing has inevitably created duplication, for which I apologize, although the more crucial points bear restatement. I recommend skimming this guide at the outset, then returning to it in detail, a section here, a section there, as your project—and expertise—progresses. Re-read the guide each year of your program because concepts that might not make sense now will soon become clear.

A note, if I may, for researchers and writers outside Europe and North America. Few social sciences graduates in Asia and South America present their work in English. I hope this guide gives you the confidence to do so because you will then be able to reach a far larger scholarly universe, while distinguishing yourself from other graduates. As the quality of your work improves and it receives the international recognition it deserves, so the prestige of your institution will rise, thereby increasing the value of your degree. Still, having spent the last two years teaching at a Chinese university, I am well aware of the bureaucratic hurdles and institutional inertia you face, and that some of my recommendations, particularly regarding library procedures and archival accessibility, are inappropriate. But providing sufficient students and faculty lobby for improvements, I am optimistic that within a few years of this guide's publication, it will be possible to request a book or roll of microfilm from interlibrary loan without paying a hefty fee, or browse through open stacks of books and government documents, or quickly access a rich array of online databases without a charge.

_____

Academics are not always rigorous in their use of professional terms, interchanging, say, *citation*, *reference*, and *footnote*, so to avoid confusion please consult the glossary at the end of the guide. Rather than fill the main chapters with clutter, I have included samples of work that illustrate key concepts and styles in a separate

Examples section; several of the samples are my own work, not from egotism but to simplify copyright issues.

If you have questions or suggestions for enhancements to the second printing, or if you spot errors that have slipped my attention then please email: m4chapman@verizon.net.

My sincerest thanks to my students for your insights; to those who provided feedback on early drafts, particularly Robert Niebuhr and Kelley Swanberg; and to you, dear reader, for buying this guide—I hope you find it useful.

MICHAEL E. CHAPMAN, PEKING UNIVERSITY, 2010

BRAINSTORMING A THESIS

"How can I possibly have a thesis when I have not even started my research," students often ask. For sure, your thesis will be a product of your research, but it would be a tragic waste of time to spend six months in the archives and a year writing a dissertation only to realize that you had not made an argument, let alone proven one. Through a process of what I call *brainstorming*, you will be able to formulate a tentative argument, or *working hypothesis* in scientific parlance, which will form the centerpiece of your proposal, guide your initial research, and develop into your final argument, although it may be that you will discard it in favor of a stronger thesis once your research is underway. But I must stress: an MA or PhD proposal without a thesis statement is not a proposal; do not begin to work in earnest until you have one. This chapter first outlines the case-study approach that your research will take, it then explains how to identify a question that your thesis will answer, and how to arrive at what engineers refer to as a *proof of concept*, and it finishes by providing a template for the essential preliminary step of writing a proposal.

CASE-STUDY APPROACH

An ideal research paper—from a thirty-page journal article to a 300-page dissertation—takes a case-study approach. While it will be about a given topic or theme, which of necessity you will need to detail sufficiently for a non-specialist reader to grasp the context, what the bulk of the paper will actually do is to document, examine, and analyze a subset of that topic. In the process, it will argue a case that supports a narrow, finely tuned, and original thesis, but, at the same time, your thesis should address a much larger, overarching argument. Your paper, then, should present a focused, detailed account of your research, based on primary-source documents, yet one that speaks to a big-picture concern.

Choose a Topic

It is more likely that you will have fallen into rather than chosen a topic. It is probable, too, that it will be an outgrowth from a previous project, in the course of which you acquired expertise. Although the topic has little bearing on a paper's quality or argument, it is advisable to consider the practical implications of your choice, on the four related grounds of interest, sources, grants, and career. First, you will devote several years to the project so it should interest you, and because you cannot complete it without guidance, it should also interest your advisor and readers. Second, if you have acquired translation proficiency in a second or third language then your topic may be contingent on research in particular foreign archives. Similarly, archival sources located conveniently close to your university or hometown may have brought a topic to your attention. Third, you may well need a scholarship or a grant, and certain topics—peace research, environmental studies, state building—attract deeper pockets. Fourth, your topic will define your career path, but predicting hot-button fields years in advance requires a crystal ball. Newly minted scholars of Islamic history were in high demand after 9/11, but they could not have foreseen this situation a decade earlier when they elected to study Arabic.

Your topic will no doubt mesh with or derive from your chosen field or methodology, to which you have gravitated on personal grounds; so many scholars of military history were once soldiers, of African American history are Black, of women's history are female, or of labor history are socialists to suggest otherwise. It may be that white historians of African slavery, or Mongolian historians of Latin America, or Catholic historians of homosexuality suffer a credibility gap when they present conference papers or apply for faculty positions. And yet, consider whether a counter-field topic would have practical merit. Good history, after all, posits objectivism. Critics would think twice before charging a Japanese scholar of Irish immigration or a Russian scholar of the African diaspora with personal bias. Good history, furthermore, depends on an original argument, and you are more likely to find one if you can keep your academic distance. So while your choice of topic does have practical considerations, do not obsess about it—save your mental energy for developing the argument.

A plea, if I may, for comparative and transnational approaches, as well as methodology, ideology, and even psychology as topic determinants. Institutions—thesis advisors and hiring committees, more to the point—cling to rigid boxes in which to study history, constructed around national boundaries and chronological eras, such as Song China or colonial America. While this pigeonholing doubtless creates specialized scholarship, it tends to preclude, or at least complicate, what are often valuable and interesting comparative studies. But even within a given box, there should be scope for lateral diversification, whether through the methods you employ, the ideologies you investigate, or the causation you attribute to your actors' agency. A study of Song China's Emperor Huizong could hinge on the topic of luxury and consumption; a study of colonial America might have for its topic the Quaker schism; a study of World War II-era Canadian foreign relations might take the psychology of Prime Minister William Lyon Mackenzie King as its topic to analyze how King's communing with the spirit world through séances affected his policymaking.

Pull—and Speed-Read—Secondary Sources

Let secondary sources provide your point of departure as well as insights into archival collections. Just as in the sciences, where a study of zooplankton motility, say, will rest on a pyramid of prior studies in marine biology, so your paper will both build on and add to the work of other historians. Having identified a dozen of the studies most relevant to your project, go to the library, which, if it is a good one, will have open stacks. Before pulling a title, be sure to spend a few minutes browsing the nearby shelves, looking in particular for books with new, unworn spines, indicating the latest scholarship. Invariably, you will spot a work that is more useful than your intended target, and which you would not have found using a keyword search of the online catalogue. Speed-reading, of which there are two basic techniques, will help you evaluate a title's worth.

To speed-read a typical 280-page monograph in about two-and-a-half hours, begin with the foreword and credits, for these can alert you to the author's personal background, intellectual mentors, economic sponsorship, and other factors suggestive of the book's viewpoint. Read most of the introduction, looking in particular for the thesis statement, then the conclusion. For each chapter, read the introductory section, then skim the body paragraphs by reading the first sentence and only continuing if the paragraph seems particularly important or interesting. As you read, take notes or annotate or both; I use a simple vertical pencil line in the outside margin, doubling the line for key points, with an asterisk for concepts. Drink caffeinated beverages and stay focused; speed-read in the morning, and never after a meal. Speed-reading is a painful process—if your forehead is not hot after half-an-hour then you are insufficiently intense—but so effective can it be that you may well realize you have absorbed the book's points far better than had you dragged it out over a week. A turbo-charged variation ideally suited for browsing stacks is to cast your eye down the center of each page; bizarre though it sounds, with a little practice this method allows you to pick up the gist of a book in five or ten minutes. Book reviews are useful adjuncts to speed-reading, although be sure to tackle them after finishing the book so you form your own judgment first. While checking for reviews in databases such as JSTOR or Project Muse, do make a point of downloading relevant review articles—those that evaluate from three to six titles simultaneously—for these both summarize the field and point the way for future scholarship.

Once you have assessed the book, turn to its bibliography. Make a note of foundational works from prior decades that you should pull later, as well as works from other fields that informed the author's methodology. Simply because an important book is not on your library's shelf is no excuse for ignoring its existence; make full use of your university's interlibrary loan (ILL) service. (In countries such as China there is an expensive charge for each ILL request, which is regrettable because it should always be a free service.) Of most immediate use when you are at the brainstorming stage will be references to primary sources—archival collections, government documents, diaries and memoirs, newspapers and magazines—both in the bibliography and more specifically in the footnotes.

Scan the Archives

You will soon reach the point when you need to explore the primary archive or archives that you have identified as crucial to your project's viability. Unless you are lucky enough to have your intended sources on microfilm or in your university's special collections, travel will be necessary, though it is sometimes practical to order photocopies of specific folders without visiting the archive, through what I call *remote control*, as described in the next chapter. To avoid duplication of effort, be diligent with note taking and citations, but scan rather than pore over the documents. All you need at this stage is a sense of what is there and, with luck, one or two smoking guns, a couple of key texts, that is, with the potential to provide evidence for an argument.

HYPOTHESIZE

It is now time to think. Think deeply, while showering, jogging, hiking a mountain, whatever helps. Think laterally—step outside the box of your received wisdom. To illustrate this critical stage in brainstorming a thesis, Hannah has enrolled at Boston College, where her field is Irish-American history, and for her doctoral dissertation has chosen to study Irish immigration, which she has further narrowed down to the Potato Famine period. But after leafing through three shelves of secondary sources in Boston College's library, and noticing four new monographs on the Famine, she felt overwhelmed. How could there possibly be anything left to say? She started, nevertheless, to work through the online finding aids of local government archives. Several hours later, she noticed a tranche of letters, diaries, and reports pertaining to an 1847 quarantine hospital on Deer Island and located in a box at the Boston City Archives. Hannah emailed the archivist, who noted in his reply that no researcher had yet requested the box. Excited, Hannah took a bus to the archive and skimmed through the folders. A letter from the island's doctor mentioning a heated debate in the newspapers caught Hannah's eye, so next day she visited the Boston Public Library to check microfilm of the *Boston Daily Advertiser* for a couple of months in early 1848.

Identify a Problem, Ask a Question, Pose an Answer

As an aid to brainstorming, down the left side of a horizontal sheet of paper, list the problems that you noticed while speed-reading the secondary sources and scanning the archival materials; think especially about contradictions, ironies, paradoxes, or *disconnects*, to use a modern idiom. What struck you as odd? What have you realized is missing from the story? In Hannah's case, she was surprised to see not only the high level of public debate over the quarantine facility, as evidenced in the *Advertiser*, but also that even Irish Bostonian elites held such divided opinions. Some wanted to send the hospital's patients back to Ireland, for they posed a genuine risk to public health, and once released would be a burden on the welfare rolls. Others wanted to welcome them as republican brothers, for Boston should be like a shining city on a hill. In a central column, write out each problem in the form of a question. Hannah wrote, "Why did Irish Bostonians, who themselves were recent immigrants, have such divided opinions, to the extent that some wanted to repatriate the new arrivals?"

Select the most pressing or troubling question. Brainstorm some more. Based on your understanding of the field from readings in the secondary literature, on the right side of the page jot down a shortlist of answers, the most plausible of which will be your working hypothesis. Ideally, it will be the single overarching argument that best ties together as many disconnects as possible. Your hypothesis, of course, will have at least one counter-argument, which you should also plan to address. A completed brainstorming chart resembles a funnel. Finally, write out your thesis statement. Hannah's was, "This dissertation will argue that public debate over the quarantine facility split Boston's Irish because it intensified their newfound Irish-American nationalism, prompting some Irish to identify with old stock Yankees." By this time, Hannah had realized that her case study of public reactions to the quarantine hospital was a subset of the much larger Nativist movement embodied in the nation-wide Know-Nothing Party. Confident about her project, she wrote, "A study of this public debate, moreover, which exacerbated racism among previously tolerant Yankee elites, will modify prevailing historiography on anti-Irish Nativism, by giving examples of Irish-American politicians who backed the Know-Nothing platform."

Note that if you cannot identify one or more counter-arguments then you do not have an argument, rather, you have an observation. Sometimes, though, it is possible to take what you thought was merely an observation and, by identifying a contrasting observation, turn it into a strong argument. Suppose I observe that Beijing's sidewalks, subways, hospitals, and other facilities are congested and overcrowded. "China has too many people," I say, implying that the government's wise one-child policy is essential to limit population growth. My friend Yang Yu then counters that narrow sidewalks are choked with street vendors' stalls and illegally parked vehicles; despite several new lines, the subway system is still inadequate for a city of twenty-two million people; and there are too few hospitals and other public facilities. "Beijing suffers from poor urban planning, lax enforcement of regulations, and a lack of investment in infrastructure," he says, implying that government officials have used China's population as an excuse to deflect criticism from unwise policies. Now the once-simple observation becomes a complex and controversial argument, as this sample thesis statement indicates: Through a comparative analysis of data from six major capital cities, this study argues that Beijing's historic overcrowding has not been an unavoidable consequence of China's vast population, but rather has resulted from shortsighted planning policies, lax enforcement of municipal codes and traffic regulations, and inadequate capital investment in essential infrastructure.

Establish Proof of Concept

Do not commit any further resources to your project, and certainly do not waste time on a proposal, until you have an established proof of concept, meaning you have sufficient evidence to indicate the feasibility of your hypothesis, as outlined in your thesis statement. Hannah had only flipped through a few folders and checked a dozen editions of a single newspaper, yet she had a proof of concept. After Boston College's dissertation committee approved her proposal, she spent all summer diligently working through three other newspapers and a range of journals, she examined records at the State House, and, with the aid of a research grant, traveled to Dublin to read letters the hospital patients sent home. But the purpose of all that work was to accumulate such a preponderant body of evidence that scholars would find it hard to challenge her original contention. Of course, just as an engineer might have discovered an unforeseen snag while putting a prototype into production, so Hannah might have found newspaper editorials that forced a modification of her argument, although it was unlikely she would have needed to abandon the project and start anew.

Design the Title

Before continuing to the proposal, and sometimes as a useful adjunct to the brainstorming process, it is important to design a working title. One school of thought maintains that the most effective titles are but a single phrase, like *Trade and Diplomacy on the China Coast*, while another holds that the title of a scholarly work needs a subtitle to provide a full description, such as *Cherishing Men from Afar: Qing Guest Ritual and the Macartney Embassy of 1793*. Bear in mind, too, that digital searches locate keywords, and you want to promote your work to the widest possible readership. Typically, the main title will be a catchy phrase suggestive of the thesis, while the subtitle will indicate the topic and period of study. After thinking about it for some time, Hannah chose a long title for her dissertation, which her advisor suggested ought to be shorter when it came time to attract a publisher. "Shining-City Nativism: Debating the Repatriation of Irish Immigrants at Boston's Deer Island Quarantine Facility, 1847–48."

WRITING A PROPOSAL

Plan to spend several weeks developing, polishing, and proofing your proposal, for it will not only be the document that convinces your committee you are ready to move forward but it will also be your calling card when you apply for grants, and provide a framework when you begin to construct the paper. You should produce three variations of your proposal. In its standard, full-length form, it will be about twelve or thirteen double-spaced pages (3,000–3,300 words), structured with six or seven subheads. In its overview form, suitable for grant applications, it will be three pages of exactly 1,000 words, with no subheads. And in its abstract form, which will be useful for promoting your project at conferences, it will be 300 words that fit on a single page.

Topic and Thesis

Beneath an **Overview** subhead, begin by clearly identifying and describing your topic. Be sure to explain its historical significance, and say why it is worth studying. You may decide to pique your reader's interest while providing a flavor of your sources by including in the first paragraph a pithy quotation from one of your actors. Effective proposals, particularly those that lay out the thesis early on, or have a complex argument, may devote 700–1,000 words to this section. Next, under a **Thesis and Its Significance** subhead, state the problem—or question—that you intend to address, and provide your tentative answer in the form of an explicit thesis statement. For greater impact, keep this section to a couple of paragraphs of less than 500 words, although your thesis will bear restating or recasting for clarity and emphasis.

Historiography: Three Uses

Beneath a **Historiography** subhead, locate your project in the relevant historiography, explaining how it will both build on and transcend that body of historical work. An ideal project fills a gap in existing literature, just as it challenges prevailing scholarship. There are three broad uses of historiography.

First, to establish legitimacy and build support. There will be a corpus of journal articles, monographs, and synthetic works relevant to your field and to your topic, all of which you should be able to discuss with authority. Remember: by the time you defend your thesis, you will be a leading expert—maybe the world's expert—on your topic, and other scholars will expect you to be capable of demonstrating that expertise, so it is vital not merely to read the prevailing works but also to keep abreast of new publications and dissertations. Your project will stand on a pyramid of knowledge, yet, at the same time, it will identify a lacuna and then fill that void. Allocate 600–1,000 words to this section.

Second, to borrow methodology that informs your approach. Suppose you are a diplomatic historian of the realist school, but your primary actor suffered from a disability that you suspect affected his judgment. As you have only a rudimentary grounding in psychology, you have identified three general works and a case study that addresses your actor's pathology.

Third, to charge at straw men. A literal straw man is a burlap bag stuffed with chaff at which soldiers run full tilt to practice bayonet thrusts. You will find it constructive to single out a work that serves as a model enemy by taking the opposite line from your argument. But be careful here, as you may make a real enemy, which is why it is prudent to attack the interpretations of retired or even deceased scholars; iconoclasm, too, can suggest that your approach is actually destructive.

Sources, Methodology, Outline

Beneath a **Sources** subhead, identify your primary sources, both archival and published; give the location of the archives or published collections and describe what they contain. A dedicated **Methodology** section is optional, typically for film or material culture studies as well as projects that rely on oral history interviews, content analysis, or cliometrics. Beneath an **Outline** subhead, include a brief, tentative outline of the written work that will result. For a research paper, perhaps an indication of the subsections may suffice, while for a dissertation provide a chapter outline or table of contents or both, giving a sense of the structure of the planned work as currently envisaged. Finish your proposal with a brief **Work Schedule**, indicating when you will conduct the various stages of research and writing, along with a target date for completion.

In finalizing the proposal, solicit input not only from your advisor, readers, and fellow students but also from instructors and mentors at a prior institution who took interest in your work; they will no doubt be pleased to hear from you and may have useful tips. Sit on the completed proposal for a couple of days before submitting it to the faculty committee members who will decide whether you are ready to begin your project.

GATHERING THE EVIDENCE

With your proposal as a template and a green light from your faculty committee, it is time to begin the long and often tedious business of evidence gathering. In part as a response to the cultural turn of the 1990s with its stress on bottom-up social history and the role of non-state actors, larger projects such as PhD dissertations increasingly tend to employ a range of sources, from oral interviews to film, which can make for a more interesting if not necessarily more cohesive narrative. Still, traditional archives are likely to supply the bulk of your evidence, so methods to facilitate the efficient processing of documents will stretch your travel budget. This chapter also emphasizes the value of detective work, and discusses the need for reliable filing systems and data handling.

SOURCES

Over the period it will take to bring your project to completion, sources will be your constant companion. As with any friendship, they will often be high maintenance. They will only work for you if you are faithful to them. You will grow to hate them as well as love them. Yet without sources, your thesis would be meaningless, so do all you can to cultivate the relationship.

Online Databases

A boon for the researcher is that archivists around the world are systematically digitizing texts, while the performance of the latest Optical Character Recognition (OCR) software is constantly improving. For a project on Boston's China trade during the Early Republic, say, it is now possible to run a keyword search across some two hundred newspapers and magazines published in towns from Maine to Rhode Island, then print or save to disk Portable Document Format (PDF) images of relevant articles. In minutes, online searches of vast databases retrieve sources that years of manual searching would not have discovered. That said, treat digitization as a tool rather than a panacea, and never as a substitute for leaving your cozy apartment. Like a hammer or a screwdriver, understand digitization's limitations as well as its usefulness. Operatives will not bother to scan damaged, incomplete, or low-contrast documents, just as blemishes, archaic typefaces, or anachronistic spelling are still the bane of OCR programs. Searching for "Congressional Session" or "Woodmass and Offley" will result in few hits if the original texts say "Congrefsional Fefsion" or "Woodmafs & Offley." Remember, too, that unless you can image full pages for an entire edition, you have to rely on the operative who entered the edition's dates and page numbers, which is why it is good practice to mention in the footnote your use of a digitized source.

Oral History Interviews

For historians of the contemporary period, oral interviews can provide not merely colorful background but also an important source of evidence. Indeed, in situations where institutional policy denies or restricts public access to crucial archives—the Archdiocese of Toledo for the 1930s, the People's Republic of China for the Cold War period, or the Walt Disney Corporation for the 1970s—oral histories may be the only source of first-hand or eyewitness information. In addition to a growing body of recorded and transcribed interviews in digital as well as book form, such as the slave narratives produced in the 1930s by the Works Progress Administration or *Blood of Spain: An Oral History of the Spanish Civil War* by Ronald Fraser, there is great value in conducting your own interviews. Some academics discount oral interviews, but providing you handle them with the same constructive skepticism with which you should approach any textual source, they can be more valuable than a letter or diary. After all, when seated alone at a desk, a writer has ample leisure to spin a tale, whereas with a recorder running and an interviewer firing questions, there is a tension akin to a courtroom's. Head off potential criticism by applying your usual academic rigor to accepted methodology.

Begin with an authority such as Donald A. Ritchie's *Doing Oral History: A Practical Guide*. Note that when your argument rests on interviews, as in a typical ethnographic study, it is best to have five or six interviewees make the same point independently before extrapolating from your subjects to a larger group. Single-subject interviews are the normal format, although there can be benefits to having one of your subject's friends participate. Being less shy, the subject forgets about the recorder sooner, while the friend serves as an aid to memory and a check on fanciful remarks.

When you pre-prepare your questions, be sure to include opening comments to identify those present, give the place, date, and time, and ask for your subjects' consent to the interview and its publication. Sound quality is important, so buy a digital recorder from a manufacturer such as Sony or Olympus, and test it at home to gain a sense of its audio dynamics. Placing the recorder on a coffee table between yourself and the interviewee is usually ideal, as is drawing curtains to soften echoic harshness. Whenever possible, upload the sound file to your laptop before you leave. Jot down proper nouns during the interview, then ask your subject to check the spellings and provide additional information at the end. Methods of transcription, from minor editing to verbatim, vary, but all are time consuming and tedious; allow a full day for every hour of interview. I err on the side of completeness, writing out every "ooh" and "um," and I include comments such as [laughs] or [fighting back tears] in square brackets.

Be aware, particularly in the United States, that human subjects have rights, which researchers must respect, and you cannot afford to embroil yourself or your institution in a lawsuit. A written consent form, detailing, at minimum, permission to cite the interview and signed by your interviewee, is always a good precaution. Check with your department if you will need the services of an institutional review board (IRB) or independent ethics committee (IEC). When protecting the identity of an interviewee with a pseudonym, mention in a footnote that, "I conducted this interview in confidentiality and have withheld the name of the interviewee by mutual consent."

Film and Material Culture

Ever since D.W. Griffith's *The Birth of a Nation* grossed $10 million at the box office in 1915, feature films have reflected as well as affected public opinion and social mores, hence their importance as sources of evidence, particularly for studies of groups with low rates of literacy. As with oral interviews, a rigorous approach should impress those who still feel that cinema is too lowbrow for academia. To put your analysis in context, try James Chapman's *Cinemas of the World: Film and Society, from 1895 to the Present*. Treat a film as you would any textual source, with faithfulness and accuracy. Transcribe your quotations directly from the actors' dialogue rather than from a screenplay or subtitles, for that is what the audience would have heard. Similarly, verify that the version you are watching has the same footage as the original release, the runtime of the film being a good indicator. I advise breaking away from the tradition of interpreting film in the present tense. Past tense will ensure your narrative's consistency, obviate awkward phrasing, and allow you to reserve present tense for distinguishing the voice of a contemporary scholar.

Material culture studies are moving out of the art history field and enriching mainstream historiography. Two edited collections provide methodological grounding: W. David Kingery's *Learning from Things: Method and Theory of Material Culture Studies*, and Thomas J. Schlereth's *Material Culture Studies in America*; consult, too, Peter Burke's *Eyewitnessing*. When you are working with museum pieces, do not take an exhibit's printed description at face value, and make a point of chatting with a subject curator.

BLITZING AN ARCHIVE

Conventional archives continue to provide the bulk of a research project's sources, if only because they contain so much untapped material. As long as households preserve family papers, celebrities and corporations have an eye for their legacy, and universities seek to expand their special collections, that situation is unlikely to change. Even if you have the luxury of staying in a friend's apartment while visiting a facility that does not restrict its hours, it is still in your best interest to blitz, as I call it, to work with efficient speed, due diligence, and above all intensity, for then you are less likely to make an error or miss an important lead. Blitzing is just as important, I suggest, when you have a grant to research abroad for an entire semester or summer, and are staying in university accommodation. Instead of relaxing carefree, set yourself a target of writing a chapter or two as well as researching. You will discover that your resulting productive attitude has created—as if by magic—more than enough time for sightseeing and socializing.

Before you Leave

Become familiar with the collection by reading the online finding aid and any overviews provided by the archivist. Always email to verify opening hours, check if you need to take special identification, and ask about policies for photocopying and photography. Use the opportunity to introduce yourself and your research interests. Archivists are busy people but they are also professionals who care deeply about their collections. After learning your needs, they will be happy to offer advice, perhaps suggesting documents in related collections that you had not thought to examine. Archives increasingly store boxes of their growing collections offsite, for which retrieval can take anywhere from a few hours to several days, so be sure to ask about this and submit an advance order if necessary.

Hotels have their highest occupancies at weekends, so search the internet for midweek specials, and, before you book, email to ask about further special pricing for students or holders of a card like the American Automobile Association's. Academic listservs and online forums that allow you to post room-wanted advertisements are an ideal way to track down cut-price accommodation in foreign countries. Gather your equipment, which should include blank paper, two quality mechanical pencils with spare leads, laptop with power supply, memory stick (flash drive) for backup plus a DVD-R disc for peace of mind, camera and ancillary items (if permissible), and a water bottle and light snack. Take sufficient cash to cover photocopying at the archive, where the desk staff are unlikely to accept a credit card. When traveling to another country, check if you will need a power outlet adapter, and whether your electronic equipment will work on a different voltage. Most power supplies for portable electronics are now self-sensing for dual-voltage (110/240V) and cycles (50/60Hz); adapter kits for multiple countries are inexpensive, although for a trip to Britain, make sure your kit includes the special three-prong adapter with large, flat pins.

On the Day

Maximize your precious time with the sources; be first in line and the last to leave. If it is your initial visit then there will inevitably be paperwork, so arrive especially early to beat the rush. Note that policies and procedures vary, particularly from country to country, and even when you inquire in advance, you may still fall foul of the system. Visiting the National Library of Ireland requires obtaining a researcher's card, for which I had brought two photographs and allowed what I thought would be ample time, but I arrived from the airport to discover that the security office had closed early for a two-hour lunch break; by the time I had my ID card, there was little time to pull folders for what was left of the afternoon. With the paperwork complete, you will need to put your things into a locker, taking only paper, pencil, laptop, and camera plus ancillary electronics with you. Do be careful—you cannot afford to make any mistakes, and you are in unfamiliar territory. At the U.S. National Archives one morning, I strode through the doors as they opened and over to the security desk, where the guard asked to see inside my laptop. As I put it down on the polished granite counter, it suddenly slid away from me, and I only just had time to slap a hand on it before it crashed to the stone floor. When my heart had settled down a few beats, I realized a janitor had sprayed silicone polish on the granite minutes earlier, and my eagerness to be first had cast me as the unsuspecting victim.

Once Inside

Snag desk space close to the photocopier, marking it with your laptop, then head directly to the counter. Providing you have already identified your first requests, immediately fill out call slips for as many boxes or folders as the limit allows; most archives require one slip per request. It may take anywhere from two minutes to two hours for the materials to arrive, so use the intervening time for setup. Check you have plugged your laptop into a receptacle that works, open up the document containing your notes, and remind yourself of the day's objectives. Once your materials arrive, you may be able to submit a second batch of requests, which means they will be waiting when you finish the first pull. Work quickly yet thoroughly. Begin by noting the document box description, then verify the folders. Remove one folder at a time, inserting a marker into the box to identify its location. Treat the documents with care, particularly if yellowing or browning indicates fragile, acidic paper. Accuracy is essential for all transcriptions. When transcribing to paper, print legibly and check each page, not just for spelling errors but also for precise punctuation; similarly, when transcribing to an MS-Word file, do not rush your typing and take the time to verify each page against the original text before moving on. Work on the basis that you will neither see the original again, nor can use the source unless its location information and transcription is exact.

Other than for essential bathroom breaks, do not stop. An occasional swig from a water fountain or, failing that, from the water bottle in your locker will keep you going, along with a snack if you must. Even when an archive closes for lunch, forswear a meal because food-induced drowsiness will waste your afternoon; use the time to process materials or prepare for the coming session. For multi-day research, fill out call slips before the last pull of the day so that you have a new batch of materials waiting for you the following morning. Before returning home, make a point to chat with the archivist or subject specialist. After hearing about your work, thoughtful curators will dig through files for reports their organization commissioned, or perhaps offer a study grant or the opportunity to give a lecture. Acknowledge, by name, the help they have provided in the credits section of your dissertation, for theirs can be a thankless vocation. A cautionary note for klepto-maniacs: stealing a document is counterproductive—how can you reference it in your work if it is not sitting in an archive?

Photocopying, Photographing, Remote Control

Some archives still do not permit copying in any form, or in-sist their reprographic department handles the job, which can ne-gate the advantages. But when you can photocopy or photograph, do so. Nothing beats photocopying because then you have a high-contrast hard copy to take with you, although at much above 20¢ per page it soon becomes costly. It is crucial to mark every page with the document's box [b.] and folder [f.] information. Failure to follow this elementary step renders the exercise useless, for how can you cite a document unless you know its precise location? When photocopying a series of pages, do number them, saving the problem of reordering them correctly if you happen to drop the sheaf.

Digital photography, at no cost per page yet with its own share of disadvantages, is increasingly practical, particularly now that facilities from London's National Archives to Budapest's Open Society Archive have installed height-adjustable camera stands. Before shelling out on a camera capable of interfacing with your laptop, understand that $500 buys several thousand photocopies, and while you can typically work quicker in the archive, reading the images later is far less convenient, and annotation requires the extra steps of processing and printing. Note, that unless you use a program like Adobe Photoshop to boost the contrast and bright-ness thereby washing out the background, all that grey will soon empty your toner cartridge. Pocket-sized point-and-shoot camer-as work fine for occasional imaging, but in production-line mode, your back will ache faster than you expected, and a dead battery will leave you stranded. Instead, invest in a high-end subcompact model (like the Canon PowerShot G-10), which has the technology to interface with your laptop but is less expensive than an SLR, while its light weight will not overbalance a desktop tripod. Invest, too, in a transformer pack so you no longer have to worry about the battery, although remember to take a small power-strip as well as an adapter for foreign receptacles. Providing the camera is steady in a tripod, brightness is less important than even illumination. Photography necessitates reliable image identification, of which there are two basic methods: first, you can place a strip of paper on the original document, giving its box and folder. Alternatively, when operating the camera from your laptop, you can dump the JPG file directly into a folder on your hard drive that you have pre-named to match the document's location; this second method is ideal for sequential records, such as a ship's logbook or a probate ledger.

When your interest is limited to a specific range of folders and the archive offers a copying service, it is sometimes worthwhile to order a duplicate of the folders' contents without visiting the archive, by what I call *remote control*. Each copy may cost as much as 50¢, and you will pay for copies of superfluous documents, but even after adding the postage, $75 for three or four folders is far cheaper than flying to a facility two thousand miles away. Researching by remote control is especially appropriate when you are trying to establish a proof of concept.

DETECTION

Effective researchers are like good detectives. For a crime such as murder, there is rarely a still-smoking gun or eyewitnesses other than the perpetrator and victim, one of whom will be unwilling to talk while the other is unable to speak. Detectives, along with lawyers and judges, therefore accept that correctly identifying and then convicting the murderer depends on building a case from pieces of circumstantial evidence, which individually mean little but collectively leave no reasonable doubt in jurors' minds. Successful detectives follow every lead however fruitless the endeavor may prove to be, think about what is missing from the scene rather than what is simply present, and check their facts carefully before filing a report that will have to withstand scrutiny in a court of law.

Following Leads

At the outset of your research, you will only have a few tentative leads, such as suggestive anecdotes, tips from other historians, and background on some actors. You may wonder how you will ever find sufficient facts to make your case. As you begin to investigate each lead, and the loose strands of evidence start to coalesce, you will uncover fresh leads with the potential for taking you into new areas of research. Indeed, it will not be long before you are facing an even more daunting problem: processing a massive amount of pertinent information. Be selective, although avoid hastily consigning leads to the trash if they are not directly relevant. Move them instead to a Pending folder, where they will be handy in the event that you later discover their importance. As an undergraduate, I had been researching a paper in the *America* magazine archive at Georgetown University, and noticed several items of correspondence with a writer whose address was in Pittsfield, Massachusetts; when I was casting around for a doctoral dissertation topic, I followed this lead, through Pittsfield to another address in nearby Lanesboro, thereby discovering 18,000 document pages of material from the 1930s in the roof of an old horse barn.

What's Missing

This point may seem foolish at first, yet it often proves to be the most vital element of successful detection. Archival research uncovers piles of material that can be as fascinating as it is beguiling. Human nature dictates that you will pore through it and write about it, perhaps obsessively. So deeply will you immerse yourself in it that you risk losing sight of the forest for the trees. Learn to stop, take a step back, and think not about what is there but about what is missing. Who, or what, is absent from the scene of the crime, and hence why? Absence, of course, is as difficult to identify as it is to document, calling for a creative approach. By way of example, I was at the Franklin D. Roosevelt Library researching Roosevelt's interest in the Spanish Civil War. At the end of the second day while driving back to my hotel, I began to think about the terseness of Roosevelt's memoranda and letters, and then about the paucity of material in general. How normal was this, I wondered. Next morning, I surprised the archivist by asking not for folders on Spain but on China, which, it soon became apparent, bulged with correspondence, including many multi-page letters from a president known for brevity. With the contrast between the two sets of files as my point of departure, I was able to build a case that Roosevelt was far more interested in exotic Asian China than he ever was in decadent Old World Spain.

Fact Checking

Nothing will devalue your project's worth, along with your scholarly credibility, faster than sloppy inaccuracies, let alone outright errors. Errors, moreover, undermine the pyramid of knowledge on which academic disciplines rest, for other researchers will draw on your work presuming it to be factually correct. Check facts—all facts—as you go, not at the end of the project when the task will be too daunting to tackle. Do not simply check dates, places, names, and events—check spellings too. Although a resource at your fingertips like Wikipedia has the merit of convenience, rely on published, peer-reviewed reference works, and, for mission-critical facts or where there is any discrepancy, corroborate with a second or third opinion. Be particularly assiduous when relying on work you conducted at an earlier stage in your training, when your self-discipline may have been lax.

OFFICE WORK

Long before a project's completion, the materials you have accumulated will become confounding. Instead of miring yourself in chaos and confusion, take the time at the outset to implement reliable systems for organizing and storing information, just as if you were an efficient office manager.

Paperwork

Cardboard archive (banker's) boxes and tabbed file folders provide an efficient, low-cost system for organizing paperwork. Set up series of folders, arranged alphabetically, for actors and archival collections, secondary-source topics, media sources, and so on, as required. Writing on the tabs in pencil allows for rearrangement or reuse. When possible, print articles and other materials double sided to save storage space. Minimize staples for multi-page documents and articles, as these will cause the folders to bulge unevenly and eventually sag.

Digital Material

Arrangements for folders and files on your computer will vary according to personal preference and the nature of the project, but this schema is typical. Within a folder for the project, create sub-folders for Articles, Data, Memos, People, and Periodicals. Within the People subfolder, create further subfolders for each major actor, where you can store a biographical file and downloaded journal articles. In addition to the master document and its backup, my main folder usually contains these MS-Word files: **Chronology**, with at least two listings for general and specific events. **Ideas**, for jotting down thoughts for later development. **Master Bibliography,** for listings of all the relevant sources. **Resources**, for details about libraries, archival collections, contacts, and journals. **Straw Men**, for arguments, pro and con, by other historians; I include quotations, double-checked for accuracy, without additional quotation marks, and footnoted with full citations so that I can conveniently cut-and-paste into my master document. **To Do**, for books to pull or request from Interlibrary Loan, articles to download, leads to follow, and corrections to make.

Be sure to backup all your files routinely to a variety of media, and retain old copies to safeguard against replacing a good file with a corrupted one. For peace of mind, nothing beats printing hardcopies. Remember, unless your laptop has a solid-state hard drive, dropping it will kill your files. At minimum, back up daily to a memory stick, weekly to a computer at a different location such as a friend's laptop or an email server, and monthly to a CD-

Rom. If you are using a desktop computer then invest in a battery backup. For MS-Word users: Options—Advanced—Save—{☑ Always create backup copy}—{☑ Allow background saves. Options—Save—{☑ Save AutoRecover information every: 10 minutes}. Do not fall into a false sense of security, for Word does not back up your work every ten minutes to a separate file, merely to a disaster recovery file, so adopt the habit of periodically clicking the floppy disk icon on the menu bar (or <Ctrl> <S>).

Spreadsheets

Other than for surveys, cliometrics, or quantitative content analyses, few historians use MS-Excel spreadsheets as a matter of routine, which is a shame for they provide utility, particularly for data that needs sorting or cross-referencing. Newspaper circulation figures, organizations and their lists of members, or signatories to a petition would all be worthwhile candidates; extra columns for *Who's Who* background on state or province, politics, religion, and so forth would then allow for convenient profiling. For actors with memberships across several organizations, say, create multiple worksheets (stacked, or three-dimensional sheets) to analyze common denominators. I had an FBI dossier of some five hundred reports, filed by eighty agents who had interviewed two hundred witnesses over a five-year period. Entering the data into separate worksheets for witnesses and agents, along with column headings for date, report number, field office, home town, organization, and so forth, admittedly took a few hours, but then it was a snap to sort and evaluate the data based on criteria such as name, date, place, or political affiliation. Simple spreadsheets, along with the other reliable office systems you have put in place, will facilitate evidence acquisition once you start the business of writing. There is nothing more frustrating than knowing you have read a quotation that at the time seemed tangential but now is vital, and yet you cannot remember where you saw it. Save yourself the aggravation of rummaging through piles of papers like a crazy person by always jotting down random observations—including the all-important reference—in your Ideas file, and storing your evidence in a logical, organized fashion.

WRITING A PAPER OR DISSERTATION

This chapter addresses the methods for and style of writing an award-winning thesis, one that will stand out as much for its flowing prose as for its persuasive exposition. You will be eager to begin, but understand that the task—particularly for a dissertation—will soon become arduous, even torturous, as you stare at a blank screen or fuss around the apartment, filled with doubts about your ability to complete one chapter let alone the entire project. Most dissertation writers start with what they consider to be the core chapter, and then use this as the basis for a conference paper and hopefully a journal article. They may then write one or two chapters that stress a particular methodology or field, such as film or gender. While this progression has practical merit, and may be inevitable, it often results in discrete chapters and a disjointed narrative. I explain later how to structure chapters, then integrate them into a seamless whole, but first I will begin at the sentence level, with an effective, modern method for presenting evidence that I call *textual immersion*, before discussing the concepts of structured précis and paragraphs as work units.

TEXTUAL IMMERSION

It will be instructive to mention two approaches to presenting and interpreting evidence within the academic disciplines of the humanities. Both have had their advocates yet both are outmoded, and they are far less effective than textual immersion. On the one hand, there are writers in the British tradition of the multi-sentence quotation, or worse, the block quotation (a lengthy extract, indented, without quotation marks). I recently reviewed a magisterial work of scholarship cast in this mold, representing two decades of prodigious archival study, yet so ubiquitous were the lengthy quoted passages and block quotes, which sometimes comprised all but three or four lines of the entire page, that there was little room left for interpretation. Instead of a work of analytical history, it read like an edited collection of primary sources. On the other hand, there are writers who follow the "thick description" approach pioneered by anthropologist Clifford Geertz. Detailed description is admirable, and Geertz could certainly bring a Balinese cockfight to life in gripping detail, yet he did so without using quotations, without presenting evidence that is, to support his assertions. Even though he stated—on quotation-less page 423 of *The Interpretation of Cultures*—that cockfighting lore was "written down in palm-leaf manuscripts," he did not quote from them. He claimed that no Balinese ever questioned an umpire's judgment nor charged a victor with unfairness, but he offered no textual evidence, such as excerpts from oral interviews. Textual immersion takes a sort of thick texting path between these two extremes, by embedding lots of short, phrase-length quotations into paraphrased, interpretive prose.

Quotations

At the heart of the system advocated here lies the phrase-length quotation, ideally a ringing phrase that best captures your actor's rhetorical style, a memorable phrase that will stick in your reader's mind, a pithy phrase that best illustrates the point you wish to make. Instead of quoting a long passage of dreary verbiage, chop out key statements and ringing rhetoric, and then paraphrase—closely, and in context—from the rest of the passage. Textual immersion is particularly effective when you devote a whole paragraph—or paragraphs—to an in-depth presentation and interpretation of a single text, such as an influential speech. Source selection is therefore important. Maybe you have five speeches by the same actor on the same subject, or several letters that make the same point. Instead of picking out quotes here and there, choose the one speech or letter that provides the richest material, and then draw intensively from it. Mastering the technique requires practice, as well as study of the kinds of quotations chosen by practitioners of the art. Study the samples in the Examples section to see how the quoted phrases and paraphrasing build up through the paragraph so that the interpretative effect is cumulative.

Textual immersion in phrase-length quotations, close paraphrasing, and cumulative interpretation offers three main advantages: First, it is easy to introduce the speaker without wasting words or disrupting the narrative flow. Second, it provides a convenient workaround for present tense, first person, or singular/plural inconsistencies. Third, it simultaneously elevates the value of the quote while maximizing space for your interpretation. After some practice, you will not only be able to immerse your reader in your actor's milieu, as if the reader were listening to the speech or thumbing through the diary, but by close paraphrasing around the quotations you will also be able to promote a step in your argument. Textual immersion lends historiography an immediacy, an intimacy that lengthy passages seem to lack; indeed, some readers admit that whenever they encounter a block quotation, they skip over it, as if its smaller typeface suggests its irrelevance.

Yet in common with many innovative, powerful techniques, textual immersion also has potentially troubling disadvantages for which you must be vigilant. Be on your guard against charges that you have put words into your actor's mouth, or selected quotations out of context or with a bias toward your thesis. One safeguard is to quote such a preponderant body of material that no critic could doubt that you had been untrue to your sources. Presenting an especially quotation-rich paragraph early in your paper will establish the method and allay fears. Be mindful, too, that a valid system for presenting primary-source quotations embedded in closely paraphrased prose can lay you open to accusations of plagiarism when applied with insufficient rigor to secondary sources. As Peter Charles Hoffer details in *Past Imperfect*, the U.S. historical profession lost credibility in the 1990s following disclosures that Stephen Ambrose and Doris Kearns Goodwin, two popular yet scholarly authors, were so prolific because they had systematically lifted entire passages from other authors, covering their tracks by changing a few words and referencing multiple pages in a footnote. Paraphrasing became a dirty word after the Ambrose and Goodwin scandals, so its rehabilitation will take time as well as responsible treatment. When you are employing a secondary source for any reason—for background information, theoretical support, or counterpoint—be cognizant that not only the source's facts but also its literary style, right down to the level of word order and selection, are the intellectual creation or property of the author. If you fail to acknowledge the provenance of either the information or the creative content, particularly if you present that content as your own work or otherwise appropriate it to your benefit, then you are stealing.

Always remember your ethical responsibilities as a professional academic. It is essential that you only quote from—and cite—a source that you have physically in front of you. In other words, never copy primary material from a secondary source and then cite it as if you were looking at the original text. By doing so, you would commit an ethical violation, and you risk discovery in the event the secondary-source author copied the quotation incorrectly or, worse, changed its meaning, both of which, I am saddened to report, I have seen on more than one occasion. So, by all means, copy from the secondary source but be sure to reference that source in the footnote. [105. Ralph T. O'Neil speaking on NBC Radio, 23 March 1931, cited in William Pencak, *For God and Country: The American Legion, 1919–1941* (Boston: Northeastern University Press, 1989), p. 79.] Alternatively, locate the original text, only do remember your ethical responsibility not to plagiarize. Were I to visit the NBC archive to copy O'Neil's remarks from the original transcript, I must still credit Pencak's research in my footnote, because I would not have found the quotation otherwise.

Despite the potential for methodological and ethical pitfalls, resist the temptation to resort to multi-sentence or block quotations. Primarily in the discipline of literary criticism but occasionally in studies of ancient history, it is traditional to begin a section with a lengthy original passage, set off as a block quotation, that subsequent body paragraphs then analyze. If your advisor or discipline insists on this method then you have little choice, although

I would urge you, nonetheless, to write the interpretive paragraphs as if the block quotation was not there. This advice holds when you are analyzing visual images—architecture, sculpture, paintings, photographs, cartoons—and of course films. Describe the image in words—bring it to life with the richness of your prose—and only include the actual image as a bonus. Then, should a publisher not let you use the image whether for reasons of space or copyright, your article still stands as written. General usage guidelines follow; for samples of textual immersion, see the Examples section.

• **Identify every speaker,** which is to say, you must introduce or attribute all your quotations. Your reader should always know who is speaking without having to search through the footnotes. Journalism is a model here because reporters understand that a quotation without attribution is next to worthless; what newspaper reader would take seriously a report that claimed, "According to an anonymous source at the Pentagon, the Canadian army is planning an invasion of Maine"? Provide the actor's full title and name at first mention in the paper or chapter, and then use just the family name thereafter. Similarly, contexts and dates should be obvious to your reader without recourse to footnotes. [Addressing West Point graduates on 1 June 2002, President George W. Bush asserted that, "Moral truth is the same in every culture."]

• **Quote mark position** is a source of confusion for many writers, due in part to variations between British and American English, as well as sloppy editing by some scholars and university presses. Yet the rules are elementary and the logic elegant. When closing a quotation, the comma or period goes inside the quotation mark. Please allow me to repeat myself: At the end of quotations, all commas and periods go "inside the quote marks." But there is an exception for other punctuation marks that you add to a quotation, although in practice you should rarely, if ever, do so. If you add a semicolon, colon, or a question mark then it goes outside the closing marks. [Begemann said, "It is such a starry night";

van Gogh wondered if she would ever come to bed.] [Van Gogh asked, "Why is it such a starry night?"] [What was behind van Gogh's question, "Why is it such a starry night"?]

- **Quote marks for quotations.** Reserve quotation marks solely for actual quotations, backed up by a footnote. That is to say, do not use them cynically to denote irony, loosely to suggest uncertainty, or irresponsibly to make an insinuation. [The "truth" about sexual pleasure is not universally available in society.] Is this author uncertain whether discussion of sexual pleasure is possible in factual terms? [Despite seizing the Philippines, Americans have never been "imperialists."] Is this author insinuating that Americans have always been imperialistic? So instead of writing, Bush was a "born-again" Christian, either state confidently—as a fact— that indeed Bush was a born-again Christian, or if the term is not yet in common usage then write that Bush was a so-called born- again Christian. To denote terms or words-as-words, use italics in- stead of quotation marks. [Bush was a self-described *born-again* Christian, someone who had experienced a spiritual rebirth.] [This paper defines *culture* as *X*.] [Cardinal Isidro Gomá used the word *red* five times in a single paragraph.] For phrases used at the time, maintain the rule by providing a supporting footnote. [On the platform were isolationists like "Radio Priest" Charles E. Coughlin.[6]] [6. For Coughlin as "'Radio Priest,'" see, for exam- ple, *Broadcasting* (15 November 1936), p. 38.]

- **Double quote marks.** Set quotations of quotations inside an extra set of marks. While this can sometimes look strange, it is grammatically precise and indicates when your source is second hand, as when you are quoting, say, a passage from a book or newspaper report that is itself a quotation. [In 1938, New York's *Herald Tribune* stressed Ellery Sedgwick's amazement at condi- tions "'in "White Spain,"'" where governance "'appeared perfect,'" prices were reasonable, food was plentiful, and Gen. Francisco Franco had "'an ambitious program of slum clearance.'"] Five marks are admittedly unusual but necessary, nevertheless, to close the quotation ending with *White Spain* because Sedgwick placed the term in quotation marks and the *Tribune's* reporter was in turn quoting Sedgwick. So to embed the quotation correctly in prose requires an outside pair of marks to denote a quotation, an inside single mark to indicate that the reporter was quoting Sedgwick, and then a double mark for Sedgwick's term. Note the logic of the double–single–double quotation-mark system that is in use in American English (it reverses in British English, with single–double–single marks).

• **Ellipses.** Use a three-dot ellipse (. . .) to denote an omission within a sentence, and a four-dot ellipse to denote the omission of one or more complete sentences. [According to John Quincy Adams, commerce was "among the natural rights and duties of men. . . . The moral obligation of commercial intercourse between nations is founded . . . upon the Christian precept to love your neighbor as yourself."] As this example suggests, ellipses create clutter and are best avoided, which is fine because textual immersion minimizes the need for them. [According to John Quincy Adams, commerce was "among the natural rights and duties of men." Based on the "Christian precept to love your neighbor as yourself," he felt that nations had a "moral obligation" to participate in commercial trade.] Do not use leading and trailing ellipses (to begin or end a sentence-length quotation). Note that when you are writing to a word limit, MS-Word counts an ellipse as three words. Ellipsis points have a space between them, so to corral ellipses that partially wrap to the next line, insert Word's special non-breaking character between each period (hold down <Ctrl> and <Shift> then press <Spacebar>).

• **Capitalization.** Rather than using a pair of fussy square brackets, or lowercasing, which is permissible, simply retain the capitalization of embedded quotations, but do change to uppercase when beginning a sentence with a lowercased quotation.

• **Errors.** Alert your reader to grammatical and spelling errors in the original text by including a [*sic*] after the problem. ["When you wanted to pack the supreme court," New York Life Insurance executive Warren R. Evans of Shelby, Montana, later wrote to Roosevelt, "you turned me from a steady supporter of yours into a cynical and disallusioned [*sic*] antagonist."] Like ellipses, every [*sic*] is a distraction, so minimize their usage, which is easier anyway when quoting short phrases. Use a 2-em-dash for missing letters, and a 3-em-dash for missing words. [According to the chronicle, "King Harold swore that Wi—— was a ———."]

Citations

Whenever you include a quotation, present information that is not common knowledge, or refer to someone else's ideas, you must provide a citation that accurately describes your source. Citations maintain the academic principles of honesty and openness, enabling other scholars to both verify and employ your research. There are two basic systems: parenthetical referencing (MLA) and footnotes (Chicago). While the MLA author-date system may have advantages for the natural and applied sciences, source information in parentheses makes prose look ugly thereby spoiling the narrative's flow, is incomplete without a bibliography, and it precludes additional information, often resulting in a mixed parenthetical and footnoted hybrid. For these reasons, MLA is—in my opinion—unsuited to the humanities, although some disciplines may still insist on its use. Chicago-style footnoting, the least intrusive and most flexible system, is now standard at leading international humanities journals.

Minor variations of Chicago style exist; I detail throughout this guide an ideal form that is suitable for all original work, as well as most article submissions, although, upon acceptance, an editor may ask for reformatting to suit the journal's style. Note: variations, as well as errors that you may see in print, do not provide a license for sloppy work. "Oh, I simply copied my style from the *Lower Tigris Geographical Society Review*," is no excuse for ignorance or laziness on your part. For sure, pick up good habits from top international journals or university presses, but let *Chicago 16th* be your final arbiter of style. If a copy is not yet sitting on your desk then postpone buying that new winter coat and order one from an online bookstore. Remember, the golden rule of style is consistency. If you are going to abbreviate *chapter* to *chap.* in footnote 4 then you must say *chap.* in footnotes 21, 37, 66, and 110 as well, otherwise your reader will have no confidence in your eye for detail, and, to quote from an old mentor of mine, "It is the details that kill you."

Best practice is to reserve footnotes solely for the information necessary to provide the citation. In other words, you should avoid extended footnotes, the logic being that if the information is important then include it in the body paragraph, and if it is not important then do not clutter up your footnotes with it, making their sheer bulk ultimately unmanageable (and un-publishable). Kevin Kenny, a senior scholar at Boston College, would relate to students in his dissertation seminar how he had once submitted an article to a journal and was humbled when one of the reviewers commented acidly that the author had a poor command of the secondary sources, as evidenced by the plethora of extended footnotes. Sometimes, of course, an extended note is necessary or desirable. You may wish to remedy confusion over an actor's name, provide the original text of a problematic translation, or include references to additional works that a reader outside your field might usefully consult. And sometimes you will include information, particularly concerning methodology or theory, in the notes of an MA thesis or PhD dissertation that you later delete from a journal article or book manuscript. Strive, nevertheless, to minimize superfluous detail in notes. General usage guidelines follow.

• **Reference number.** Insert a footnote reference number— a superscripted Arabic numeral—at the end of the sentence containing the referent. Note that the reference number goes last, outside all marks. [During a speech to unveil a statue of Simón Bolívar in 1921, President Warren G. Harding averred that the New World "miracle" was part of a "divine plan," a "supreme scheme for developing civilization."[13]] ["Censorship is necessarily a blunt instrument," writes film studies scholar Kevin Rockett, an "attempt at total repression" by state officials.[24]] MS-Word has an automatic function for creating footnotes, although its default parameters bear improvement. In particular, in the footnote itself, remove the footnote number's superscripting and follow it with a period and then two spaces; for convenience of formatting, I invariably cut-and-paste footnotes. Reset footnote reference numbers (to 1) at the start of each new chapter.

• **Reference information.** Footnotes credit the author in given-name, family-name format, and set details of publication inside parentheses, as distinct from bibliographies, which alphabetize authors in family-name, given-name order, and provide publication information in discreet sentences. [13. Warren G. Harding, speech, Simón Bolívar Statue unveiling, *New York Times*, 20 April 1921, p. 2.] [24. Kevin Rockett, *Irish Film Censorship: A Cultural Journey from Silent Cinema to Internet Pornography* (Dublin: Four Courts Press, 2004), p. 13.] Asian authors whose family name comes first—Wang Xiaoyu—appear the same in footnotes and bibliographies, unless the author has adopted a Western-style name order.

• **Italicize published works.** This logical rule determines whether, and what part of a work's title appears in italics. In both footnotes and running text, set the title of any published work in italics, including books, journals, newspapers, plays, films, operas, and musical scores. [*War and Peace. Journal of Military History. New York Times. Hamlet. The Empire Strikes Back. Aida. Horn Concerto in No. 2.*] Conversely, the title of any unpublished work appears in roman type enclosed in quotation marks, including classified government reports, association minute books, memoirs, and PhD dissertations. ["War Plan Green." "Portland Elks Lodge Minutes, 2008." "My Nile Cruise, 1956." "Salsa in Santa Cruz: An Ethnography."] Titles of articles in a journal, or chapters in an edited collection, similarly appear in roman enclosed in quote marks, because it is the journal or book that is the published work. ["Zhou Enlai and the Bandung Conference," *Journal of Cold War Studies*.] [Zuckermann's narrow study, "Pencil Buildings of Saigon," appeared in Shi Guanhua's magisterial *Architecture of Southeast Asia* in 2005.] It is clear from the typeface, therefore, whether a given title is that of a published work; a book with an ISBN number or a sixteen-page pamphlet printed in the thousands are easy to categorize as published, but less so would be thirty photocopies of a club's annual newsletter.

• **Short form.** Give the source in full for the first citation, and then in concise form (short form) for the second and subsequent citations. [27. Rockett, *Film Censorship*, pp. 119–20.]

• **Page numbers.** Give a single page in the form p. 22. To save space, many journal and book publishers omit the p., but you should include it in your manuscript to avoid confusion with other numbers, such as newspaper sections or government documents. Give two or more pages in the form pp. 6–8. Notice the use of an en-dash to denote a number range, in this case meaning *from* 6 *to* 8, and that there must be a single space after a p. or pp. For sentences containing two or more quoted phrases from different pages, list the page numbers in the footnote in the form pp. 256, 271. For those rare sentences containing two or more quoted phrases from different works, create a compound footnote with the references separated by semicolons.

• **Newspapers.** When citing newspaper sources, always include page numbers (column position is unnecessary). Be on your guard for multiple daily editions and page numbering across multiple sections. For consistency, italicize place of publication even if the city or town name is not part of the masthead. [29. *New York Herald Tribune*, 22 March 1938, morning edition, section IV, p. 22.]

• **Bibliography.** For projects requiring a bibliography—senior research papers, MA theses, PhD dissertations—every time you cite a new work be sure to add it to the bibliography, for this will save heartache at your project's completion. Most departments insist that the bibliography must contain—but only contain—any work cited in the footnotes, which is to say, do not pad the bibliography with works you have read but not cited. See the Examples section for bibliographic categories and sample entries.

• **Endnotes.** Unless a journal or press insists, always use footnotes rather than endnotes; footnotes not only make references accessible to your reader but when they are staring at you on the page they also discourage bad habits, like formatting them sloppily or turning them into essays.

Plug in the Actors

Even world-renowned scholars, most commonly in the fields of political science and international relations, make statements like, "After Germany invaded in May 1940, France confronted a dilemma," or "Once Beijing had sent in the PLA, America could only frown self-righteously on China's policies." Germany invading, France confronting, Beijing sending, and America frowning paint history in strokes the size of a street sweeper. As soon as you start the process of replacing geographic entities, which have no capacity for thought let alone facial expressions, with organizations, you will have to admit that those organizations in turn consisted of actors who did not always think or express themselves in lockstep. Perhaps most of the three million soldiers of the *Wehrmacht*'s Army Groups A, B, and C were intent on exacting vengeance for the Clemenceau government's punitive terms at Versailles in 1919. But during their May 1989 meetings in Beijing, members of the Chinese Communist Party's politburo were far from unified over their response to the Tiananmen protest movement, to the extent that paramount leader Deng Xiaoping ousted Zhao Ziyang, the Party's reformist secretary-general, from his post. Plugging in the actors necessitates a lot more research, and will no doubt lengthen and complicate the project, yet it results in a different story, one that satisfies for its richness and nuance.

Actor-centric exposition raises the issue of viewpoints. Ideally, each body paragraph should contain only one viewpoint, that is, the thoughts, words, or deeds of a single actor. In a paragraph about Hitler dawdling over Operation Citadel, a pivotal battle at Kursk in July 1943, if you have just said, "He listened carefully to Manstein, yet he also factored Keitel's optimism into his calculations about a suitable launch date," then do not also go on to say, "Keitel, who habitually underestimated Soviet strength, felt that

Hitler had obfuscated long enough." Your argument will gain weight and intelligibility if you break out what Keitel was thinking into a second paragraph. Authors of multiple-viewpoint mystery novels follow this method, ensuring that each chapter never has more than a single knower. Similarly, make certain that your reader can distinguish between the statements and thoughts of your actors and your own interpretation and analysis. Indeed, the pitfall of textual immersion lies in its power to convince, so you need to be particularly careful to distance your voice from those of your actors. One approach is to confine your opinion to the closing sentences of each paragraph, but for maximum separation, break out your interpretation into a second paragraph.

Banish the Passive Voice

Effective textual immersion in your actors' lives depends on the active voice. Again, even though some famous scholars, particularly European ones, bask in the anonymity of the passive voice, you have no excuse to follow suit. Old fashioned and woolly, the passive voice not only lengthens sentences but also masks actors and shifts responsibility. Especially with the increasing focus on bottom-up social history, it is critically important to identify your actors. "The Kongolese were converted to Christianity." Fine, but who converted them? "Portuguese missionaries converted the Kongolese to Christianity," is an adequate, active-voice explanation, but one that nonetheless places the onus on outside agency. Were the Kongolese mute and despondent subjects, or were they active, enthusiastic participants, dancing and singing for their newfound spirituality? "Attracted by Christianity's liberating message and clear-cut monotheism, the Kongolese flocked to the Portuguese missions seeking conversion," shines the spotlight squarely on the Kongolese. "Priests were murdered in Toledo." Yes, they were, but who did the deed? Revised to active voice, the actors become explicit: "Anarcho-syndicalists murdered priests in Toledo." "Of the four million dollars received by Lengthy Life, only a million was paid out to claimants." Revision to active voice identifies the payer and saves three words: "Lengthy Life received four million dollars yet only paid out a million to claimants." Uncertainty or ignorance is no excuse for passive voice constructions, because MS-Word will automatically alert you with its green wavy line, providing you check the "Passive sentences" box in the Grammar and Style settings section of Options. Banish the passive—be active. Always think: who is doing what to whom.

STRUCTURED PRÉCIS

Joining words into sentences, melding sentences into paragraphs, and arranging paragraphs into a narrative necessarily creates ever larger—often jumbled and verbose—blocks of text. Two features of the system I advocate will help you to order the chaos and trim the clutter: solid, explicit structure, teamed with tight, précised prose. *Structured précis*, as I call the resulting method, may appear overly formulaic to some readers and too dense to others, yet critics will have no difficulty navigating your narrative, just as the power of your thesis will not fail to impress them, packed as it is into such an accessible space.

Paragraphs as Work Units

Body paragraphs have a lot of work to do. They should begin with a topic sentence, present and interpret evidence in order to make a point that contributes to the larger argument, and end with a summation or conclusion before transitioning smoothly into the next body paragraph. Consequently, the most effective of them will be on the long side, around 250–300 hundred words, sometimes even longer than 350 words. Note that unless you are a journalist or a novelist, two sentences do not constitute a paragraph. To take a body paragraph's elements in turn, the topic sentence introduces the paragraph and suggests or describes its function in the context of your thesis; a paragraph without a topic sentence will lack purpose and lack direction. Regard topic sentences as miniature thesis statements. Best practice is to concentrate the evidence early in the paragraph and then build up the interpretation toward the end. Strive to avoid ending a paragraph in a quotation; on the rare occasion when I do so, the following paragraph is substantively interpretive and the closing quotation reiterates or emphasizes the evidence presented beforehand. Use the last sentence, sometimes two, to summarize the paragraph's point, and, ideally, wrap back to the topic sentence by including one of its key words or phrases. In the closing sentence or the first part of the next paragraph's opening sentence, engineer a transition, typically by repeating a phrase or concept from the two parts, whether idiomatically or as a literal repetition of a word. Each paragraph should connect with and flow seamlessly into its neighbor, building the thesis from a succession of related points. To test whether you have made the paragraphs in a given section hard-working members of your project, try giving each one a temporary subhead of no more than eight words that describes its function. If reading through the subheads explains the section's purpose and argument then you have been successful. But if you struggle to summarize a paragraph's function, or the subheads, taken together across the paper, do not make sense in light of your thesis, then it is time to rethink the structure and rework the paragraphs.

Road Maps

Jumbled argumentation and stream-of-consciousness prose have no place in academic writing. If you are one of those creative types then remember that structure is still your friend. Even James Joyce's apparently formless *Ulysses* conformed to a plan. Err on the side of more structure, not less, because it is easy to replace "First . . . Second . . . Third" constructions with something less boilerplate, but making sense of chaos after the fact will rarely prove satisfactory. Editors of certain journals may ask you to remove subheads, but they will simply reject your submission out of hand if it is unstructured. From the outset, therefore, write with explicit confidence, not implicit vagueness.

Solid structure begins with this overarching schema: introduction, three to five main points, conclusion. By *main point*, I mean the primary components of your thesis (argument), the points that someone listening to a twenty-minute conference paper about your research would remember the next day. This structural schema operates primarily at the body-paragraph level, though the value of its logic applies just as well at the micro level of sentences and the macro level of multi-chapter dissertations. An ideal research paper of 6,500 words, or a somewhat longer dissertation chapter of 9–11,000 words, opens with three or four introductory paragraphs, contains four to six subheads beneath each of which follow the body paragraphs that present and interpret the evidence necessary to make each main point, and closes with a couple of concluding paragraphs. Having laid out your thesis in the introduction, miss no opportunity to reinforce it point by point and paragraph by paragraph; work at giving each main point its own mini thesis statement, and each paragraph a topic sentence that is itself a subset of the thesis. Following the same schema, each sub-headed section should also open with a paragraph of an introductory nature that sets up the section's main point; it may well contain three to five body paragraphs that make respective sub-points; and its closing paragraph will offer an interim conclusion. Toward the end of each concluding paragraph, whether at the paper/chapter or main-point level, tie back to one of the introduction's key phrases, thereby completing the rhetorical circle.

No introduction is complete without a road map, preferably an explicit one, situated toward the end of the last introductory paragraph, which lists the main points (subheads) in their respective order, often with a word or two of explanation. Road maps provide a set of directions so that the reader knows what to expect at each junction and thereby does not become lost. Simplified versions of the road map concept also work at the paragraph level. Note here the importance of confident, explicit constructions. Inexperienced writers and even some old hands say things like, "There were many reasons why X happened, including . . ." or "There are several explanations for Y." Yes, of course there were. There may indeed have been twenty possible reasons for X and fifty explanations for Y. But you are the expert—you have studied the documents and formed an opinion. It is your job to choose a manageable number (three to five) of the most important reasons or explanations and present those to your reader. "*X* happened for three main reasons: First, . . . Second, . . . Third, . . ."

Practice the Fine Art of Précis

Lost art may be more apt, as few high schools today include methods for shortening written passages in their language curricula. A classic précis exercise requires taking a passage of a given length and rendering it in half as many words, without sacrificing content or meaning. Précis does not merely save words. It concentrates argument. Cutting out the clutter makes it easier for a reader to grasp your point. Writing long—as most writers do—is fine for a first draft, providing you then take time to précis, which may mean double the first draft's completion time. Effective précis comes only with practice, in part because every writer has a unique style, so certain techniques will pay greater dividends than others.

Précis embodies four main techniques: First, move to a longer, more complex sentence structure, concatenating adjacent sentences that say more or less the same thing; sentences that begin with pronouns, especially *This*, are likely candidates. Aids to multi-clause sentences are semicolons and em-dashes in pairs, although limit these constructions. Second, experiment with changing the order of phrases. Beginning some sentences with a participial or gerund phrase typically saves a few words, but again, this is a tactic best not overused. Third, cut out 90 percent of adverbs and adjectives—hackneyed words like *very* are useless anyway—save their power for special effect. Fourth, avoid stating what is obvious to your reader. Instead of writing "the United States," write "America"; better still, if *America* is implicit, remove the reference altogether. Take every opportunity to cut superfluous words. Say either "during the time" or "during the period" but never "during the time period," which would be redundant. Look for two or more words you can replace with one, such as *prior to* with *before*, *at the present time* with *now*. There are usually alternatives for phrases like *as a result of*, such as *because of* or *consequent to*, and "in the process of" is unnecessary verbiage that you can simply jettison.

POLISHED PROSE

You now have an introduction with its thesis statement and road map; you have sub-headed sections, each of which makes a main point that advances your thesis through textual immersion in lots of skillfully interpreted, evidentiary quotations embedded in your prose; and you have a conclusion that reinforces the thesis while tying back to the introduction. But do not think for a moment that it is therefore time to relax. Just as in the production of a jade vase or silver chalice, you must now begin the exacting yet essential work of polishing, without which your exposition would be no more a work of art than any piece of grey stone or tarnished metal.

Scholarly Style

Your strategy should always be to gain recognition through quality—original research, polished prose, powerful argumentation—not glitz or gimmickry. Remember: nothing undermines quality and negates the hundreds of hours you devoted to your project faster than inconsistency, errors, and general sloppiness. Peppering your paper with spicy colloquialisms or printing it in a fancy font will distract your reader, detracting from your scholarship, not adding to it. Understand that there are internationally accepted standards, as outlined in *Chicago 16th* and reinforced in this guide. Despite what you may hear or see to the contrary in certain classrooms or publications, learn and implement those standards. Yet even within the ivory tower's established conventions, there is nonetheless plenty of scope for individuality and creativity, but it does take considerable time and effort to develop a rich, flowing scholarly style. By really working at your style, it will develop before you know it. Save old papers, re-read them a year later, and you will be amazed at your improvement. A plea: popular modern languages, such as Chinese, Spanish, and particularly English, are dynamic, so, as you progress through the education system and down the path of your chosen career, keep abreast of current trends and usage; writing is far too vital a form of communication for your style to become passé.

When scholars write for their peers, their prose can seem turgid, pedantic, and even downright unreadable to history buffs who eagerly buy the latest best-sellers often penned by erstwhile journalists. Scholars, perhaps in part from envy, scorn popular writers for their lack of academic rigor, yet there is no reason why serious historiography cannot also be enjoyable to read. Still, it is easy to cross the line from acceptable scholarly style to chatty, cliché journalese, just as it is tempting to demonstrate erudition by including jargon that requires a dictionary to translate. Work at finding a middle ground, with *work* being the operative word. Above all, treat your writing as an art form, like a painting that could always have been better, and will be when the artist begins the next canvas. Do not make the mistake of thinking that brilliant writers have a natural talent, one you could therefore never hope to emulate. Brilliant writing is invariably a product of hours of work, hard work devoted to polishing prose until it sparkles. Please study this guide's Grammar and Style Essentials, as well as Strunk and White's still excellent *Elements of Style*, and note these additional points:

• **Gambits.** Just like the first bars of a Rolling Stones song, a sentence's opening gambit sets the stage for the drama to come. Work to make your gambits as interesting and different as possible, especially for the all-important first sentence—usually the topic sentence—of a paragraph. If you are beginning every third or fourth sentence with *The* then you are probably writing banal, unimaginative English. Notice how something as apparently simple as changing how you start a sentence has repercussions that fundamentally alter your style. Five years ago, I decided that I would never begin a sentence with *The*, a promise I have not yet broken, even in emails. Perhaps this writing trait is a silly eccentricity or conceit, and yet implementing it forced me to spend time thinking about word order and selection, phrasing, and sentence construction in general. As a result, my style certainly evolved, though whether it improved I leave to my reader to decide. But dislike my style as you may, please accept my challenge, which is to work constantly and consciously on your own style to make it more effective, interesting, and readable.

- **Personal pronouns.** Be sparing with personal pronouns; when necessary, use *one* but not *you* or *we*. Limit the first person *I* to occasional use in introductory paragraphs and interpretational or argumentative constructs. Keep your academic distance: write, "Americans invaded Iraq," not "we invaded Iraq."

- **Forensics.** Do not impose your argument on your reader with statements like, "We can see that Wilson was an arrogant racist." Instead, say, with confidence, "Wilson was an arrogant racist," or perhaps, "Wilson, as the evidence indicates, was an arrogant racist." Similarly, do not hide your opinion behind statements like, "One might argue that Wilson should have recognized the Soviet Union." If that is indeed the argument you wish to make then say so, because one might just as easily argue the opposite. "Wilson, I argue, should have recognized the Soviet Union." Work to balance your style of argumentation between excessive caution and overconfidence. When you begin writing your first major research project, incomplete evidence or just simple hesitancy will prompt you to hedge your bets with *perhaps* and *maybe*. Once your evidence comes together, your confidence grows, and you scan through completed chapters for iterations of such fence-sitting words, you may realize that they were only serving to confuse your reader and devalue your point. Yet avoid making definitive claims when the supporting evidence is circumstantial or flimsy.

- **Emphasis.** Banish superlatives, exclamation marks, words like *fantastic, amazing, great,* and especially that much overused and wasteful word, *very*. Strain not to add emphasis (italics), whether to your own prose or to quotations. Instead, stress your points through the power of vocabulary. "It was cold on the summit of Mount Washington," sounds just as foreboding as, "It was very cold on the summit of Mount Washington." For those occasions when you can afford an extra word to make a point: "It was bitterly cold . . ."

- **Past tense.** Write entirely in the past tense, except to distinguish the work of a contemporary author on which you are drawing.
- **Contractions.** In formal academic writing, do not use contractions like *can't* and *won't*. Some scholars occasionally drop a contraction or two into a book-length work, but for effect rather than from nonchalance.
- **Vocabulary.** English has a rich vocabulary so there is no excuse for using vague or ugly words like *got*. [Smith wrote the letter when he got home.] [Smith wrote the letter when he returned home.] *Got* is often redundant anyway. [John got married to Susan.] [John married Susan (and saved two precious words).] Avoid all but the choicest colloquialisms, and then use them for effect or emphasis. Reword sentences that end in prepositions or include ghastly constructs like *had had*.
- **That** is no mere conjunction. It is a key pointing word the importance of which increases with sentence length and complexity, so strive to have never more than a single *that* in any given sentence. Upon writing a sentence with two *that*s, sit back and decide which of the clauses carries the most weight (the one you are most concerned to point to) and then recast the other *that* clause, perhaps to a gerund. [Smith wrote a letter that contained all the proof that Brown sought.] [Smith wrote a letter containing all the proof that Brown sought.] Because it adds precision and therefore enhances readability, err on the side of using more *that*s than less, at least before you enter serious précis mode. In the last example, *that* is optional, and perhaps unnecessary, but only because the sentence is so simple. [Smith wrote a letter containing all the proof Brown sought.]
- **Triplets** have an appealing esthetic, whether at the sentence level or in the case of three main points, but as with all stylistic devices, avoid overuse by employing doublets and occasional foursomes. [Because of the restless intellects, principled values, and disciplined work habits of those who quarried its stone and stacked its blocks, the ideology that the Monument embodied—

and hence the kind of national identity it had the power to create through symbolism and myth—began to change.]

- **Cadence.** Certain words and phrases can develop a pleasing rhythm or cadence, just as other words sound downright ugly as they roll off the tongue. Try reading passages aloud to see how they sound, and experiment with interchanging words with similar meanings but different syllabic length. Alliteration is an equally important component of esthetically pleasing prose.

- **Tempo.** Parameters—over which you have considerable control—such as word choice, punctuation, and sentence length dictate the tempo of your writing, and hence the emphasis you decide to give to particular interpretive or argumentative passages. Sometimes you will wish to move your readers along, smoothly at a brisk pace, through evidentiary material. At other times, perhaps when you make a key observation or conclusion, it may be best to slow your readers down, bring them to a halt, or even force them to re-read a passage. *Although* reads slower than *though*, *still* reads quicker than *nevertheless*, and *but* reads quicker than *yet* despite being the same length. Many readers habitually stop at the word *paradox*, reading the passage a few times to ensure they have correctly solved the riddle. Adding optional commas slows the pace and creates a measured tempo. [She sprinted toward the president and from less than fifty feet opened fire.] [She walked deliberately toward the president, and, from less than fifty feet, opened fire.] Similarly, adding "on the one hand . . . on the other hand" or "not only . . . but also" phrasing costs extra words but increases emphasis. [Yet Doyle was an influential Catholic and a Loyalist sympathizer.] [Yet not only was Doyle an influential Catholic but he was also a Loyalist sympathizer.]

- **Metaphors.** Good writers take the time to invent metaphors and similes to make memorable otherwise lifeless passages. You may find George Orwell's provocative essay, "Politics and the English Language," to be a source of inspiration.

- **Chronological sense.** Writing about the past invariably involves discussing events that occurred before or after other events, relative to a particular moment. Be cognizant of the need to present the train of events so that your reader can sense the chronology, thereby appreciating the significance of the events as a whole. *Had* is essential for this purpose, though its use is often optional; I lean toward overusing *had*, at the risk of producing boring prose. [By 3 PM, Howe had prepared his attack. Sniper fire from barns to his left had forced him to order the frigates in the Charles River to lob incendiaries, and now smoke was wafting over the battlefield from the burning town. His reserve had disembarked, and he could count on around 3,500 men. Gen. Robert Pigot would mount the frontal assault on the redoubt, while he would lead the grenadiers against the rail fence.] This example orders events either side of *now* (at 3 PM); the following example tells the same story in eleven less words yet conveys little sense of chronology. [At 3 PM, Howe mounted his attack. Sniper fire from barns to his left forced him to order the frigates in the Charles River to lob incendiaries. Smoke wafted over the battlefield from the burning town. His reserve disembarked, giving him around 3,500 men. Gen. Robert Pigot mounted a frontal assault on the redoubt, while he led the grenadiers against the rail fence.]

• **Creative writing.** Some paragraphs, typically those of an interpretive or concluding nature, will benefit from a more creative treatment. I do not wish to offend social sensibilities, so I will confine this observation to personal experience, that while I write better analytical paragraphs after a breakfast mug of strong black coffee, my creative writing blossoms over an evening glass of well-aged red wine.

• **Consistency.** Remember the golden rule of style: be consistent throughout. If you are using em-dashes in pairs—to demarcate sub-clauses—then avoid having a sentence with a single em-dash at the end; use a semicolon instead. Introduce the reader to your style early on. If you like to break up the occasional sentence with a semicolon then avoid waiting until the fourth paragraph before throwing in three of them back-to-back. Work to gain and hold your reader's confidence.

- **Experiment.** Grammarians' rules are ultimately no different from others that occasionally one may break to advantage, and English, as a popular global language, is anyway perpetually in flux. So when you have a good reason, or are feeling particularly confident, by all means try an experiment, but be sure to break with convention by design rather than from ignorance.

Building the Argument

Précising paragraphs and polishing prose go hand in glove with building your argument. Cut the clutter, streamline the remainder, and sharpen the points. You may well notice that as your research and interpretation progresses, and in light of your particular methodological approach, your topic has narrowed to a subset of the original topic while your thesis has broadened into a powerful—and hopefully unique—overarching argument. In the case of my own doctoral dissertation, what began as a working thesis became one of three subsidiary arguments that supported a new thesis. Yet with every completed chapter, problems of clarity and continuity multiply amid the project's increasing complexity. No longer an amateur researcher, you have become a professional project manager, and, as such, you should employ all the tools and assistance available.

One useful tool is MS-Word's Document Map feature, an icon for which I keep handy on my toolbar. Set up each subhead at Level 2 and each chapter at Level 1 (as in the MS-Word Settings section), then click the icon to instantly see and navigate through your project's structure. At the same time, take a mental step back from your project to think deeply but with detachment about the function that each chapter, section, and even paragraph performs. How does each component advance your thesis? Still, the close involvement that comes with being a researcher/writer can make it difficult, if not impossible, to evaluate your own work. It is therefore essential to enlist the assistance of as many readers as possible, in addition to the members of your dissertation committee. You will find few people more willing to help than your peers, so join a departmental writing group, or, better still, form your own group with half-a-dozen fellow students. Meet each month, with two presenters circulating a chapter a few days in advance. Best practice is for every member to line edit (proofread) each presentation, which establishes a quid pro quo that all members will come to value despite the extra work entailed. Even if you meet in a restaurant over a couple of beers, maintain a collegial atmosphere; consider the black-box approach, with each member offering a critique and the presenter waiting dispassionately until the end before responding. Peer pressure to present will not only improve the quality of your work but also enhance productivity. In contrast to conference commentators or even busy dissertation advisors, group members soon develop an appreciation, chapter by chapter, of how your entire project hangs together.

Novice writers typically begin a new chapter with a new MS-Word document, and some continue until the project's completion on a document per chapter basis. While it is easier to circulate chapters if they are in discrete documents, and one does not have all one's digital eggs in the same electronic basket, the pros of this method lag far behind the cons. To facilitate the melding of chapters into a seamless whole, thereby ensuring your project's continuity and forensic power, migrate individual chapters to a single-document format as soon as possible. With everything under a single roof, you will be able to make full use of tools such as Document Map, scan for duplicate words and phrases, and develop smooth chapter transitions. Each chapter should build on the work of its predecessor while introducing and developing a new main point, perhaps in the context of an actor or an event. Maintaining continuity with and relevance to the main points in adjacent chapters, within an explicit framework that advances your argument step by logical step, will obviate admissions of structural failure like, "as I showed in chapter three." Once you have a few chapters in place, and thought about the connections among them, try adding mini road maps to the last sentence of each chapter's conclusion, thereby preparing your reader for what follows on the next page.

Print–Edit–Review Cycle

Over time, every writer comes to favor certain words, phrasing, and literary constructions, which harmonize into a characteristic style. Developing a signature style is as important as it is valuable, and yet good writers will guard against banal repetition or over usage. Repetition, of course, can be effective, to wit Martin Luther King's memorable "I Have a Dream" speech, but practice the art intentionally, not accidentally. Look back at the Consistency bullet on page fifty-one. Did I really intend to write two "If you . . . then avoid" sentences hand running? Well, actually not when I first wrote them, but having spotted the issue, I decided to make it a feature, which is why I followed the second iteration with a short maxim-like sentence about one's reader so as to mirror the prior construct. I admit, nonetheless, to an over reliance on *if . . . then* sentences (made the more obvious by my inclusion of *then* after every *if,* in order to stick with standard constructions), which borders on an addiction.

Spotting structural and stylistic issues, such as transitions and duplicate phrasing, is problematic when scrolling a video screen. Experiment with MS-Word's Draft view as well as the more popular Print Layout, and consider investing in a twenty-two-inch-plus display set vertically (in portrait mode) so that you can scan up and down multiple pages without scrolling; LCD displays have come down in price, and many now have built-in pivots to allow for easy rotation. To maximize my vertical display while composing as well as editing, I use Draft view and minimize my toolbars. To check for correct spacing between words, particularly in footnotes where there are so many abbreviations, toggle MS-Word's Show/Hide feature, for which I keep an icon on my toolbar, but there is also a hotkey: <Ctrl> <Shift> <*>. When editing footnotes, zoom in to 140 percent so that punctuation appears larger than regular 12-pt type. Still, even the biggest digital display will always impose severe limitations, so at the core of any method for producing quality written work lies what I call the print–edit–review cycle. At this stage, which should begin at the completion of your first draft, if not before, temporarily override academia's dou-

ble (28-pt) line spacing in order to boost the lines-per-page thereby enhancing readability, and print double-sided to save paper.
Staple the stack at the top left corner, arm yourself with a mechanical pencil, and take every opportunity—subway, walking, meal-
times—to line-edit the printed pages. Check, particularly, for unusual words that you have used more than once, as well as common words and phrasing that you are overusing. Ensure that you
give names in full at first mention and then just family name thereafter. Check the footnotes for errors too, because it will take several passes before they are perfect. When you are through, review
your edits on-screen, making full use of MS-Word's thesaurus to
obviate duplicate words and add variety to your prose. Repeat the
cycle as often as it takes to produce structured précis, polished
prose, and an error-free publishable copy.

COMPLETING THE PROJECT

Guides like this one, I fear, make everything sound too easy.
Few people write dissertations and even fewer see them in print,
which indicates how difficult the process actually is. There will be
times when you question whether your argument makes any sense,
times even when you feel like starting over or quitting altogether.
Yet such self doubt can be constructive, for overconfidence breeds
complacency and hubris. But even when everything is going well
and you are close to completing the project, every so often, put a
few hours aside for introspection.

Introspection

Anxious thoughts scamper around the brain like a gerbil on a
treadmill. Try marshaling them in a one- or two-page memo or
think-piece. Looking back through my files, I see there were seven
occasions when I felt a need to commit my worries to paper, then
email the resulting think-piece to my advisor and readers for feedback. I usually caught them at a busy time, and sometimes their
advice was brief, but the exercise always helped me over a difficult
patch, or allowed me to understand, if not always solve, a complex
problem. By chapter five, I was grappling with how to apply post-

modernist theory and explain how it affected my actors' world-view. As the stack of specialized works on my desk grew, the faster the gerbil scurried. At a loss, I worked up a thoughtful think-piece and emailed it to Paul Breines, Boston College's legendary intellectual historian. "F--- theory," was his characteristic reply, by which he meant that I should not obsess over how to incorporate post-modernist deconstruction techniques into my dissertation because the solid theoretical grounding I had just demonstrated to him in the think-piece would naturally inform my interpretation. Marshaling what previously had been random thoughts into order in the think-piece, and then soliciting advice, helped me to understand the theory and saved my dissertation from a plague of tedious jargon.

Concluding Steps

Once you have completed all the chapters (or body paragraphs in the case of a research paper) and run them through the print–edit–review cycle several times, you will be ready to write the conclusion. A good conclusion not only sums up the evidence and reinforces the thesis but also stresses how the thesis informs and modifies prevailing scholarship. Ideally, it will point the way to further research and directions that the field might take in the future. Then, revisit the introduction, as you may already have done several times since the project's inception. My dissertation's introduction required a complete rewrite, although whether that indicates a vindication of the scholarly process or a failure of vision on my part I am unsure. During the ongoing print–edit–review cycle, which can now include the conclusion and revised introduction, implement the following:

• **Ibid.** Change consecutive footnote references to the same work to ibid., and, where applicable, to a consecutive author to id.

• **Compound footnotes.** If you intend to use compound footnotes, with a single note at the end of each paragraph containing the citations for all of that paragraph's sources, then this is an ideal time to migrate the individual notes to the compound format.

- **Resets.** Verify that you have reset all shortened names, abbreviated organizations, and concise (short form) footnote references to their full-length state at their first mention in every chapter. It is good policy not to make exceptions, even for organizations as commonplace as the United Nations (UN) or Federal Bureau of Investigation (FBI), if only to indicate to your reader that you are as consistent as you are conscientious. Strike a balance between banal repetition and saving words on the one hand and losing your reader on the other hand. Having first mentioned "President Franklin D. Roosevelt" on page two of a forty-page chapter, you are unlikely to lose your reader by using the "Roosevelt" short form on pages ten, twenty-two, and thirty-five. But for an obscure actor that you reference on page five and then not again until page thirty, provide most of the name if not all of it. Sgt. Edwin L. Parker Jr. could be Sgt. Edwin Parker at second mention.

- **Bibliography.** Providing you added to your bibliography each time you referenced a new title, all that is necessary here is to include it in the print–edit–review cycle, but pay attention for any titles that should not be in the bibliography because you dispensed with the reference. Standard practice is to include only those works in the bibliography for which there are citations in the text.

- **Front matter.** Where applicable, compile a table of contents, and write the acknowledgements, copyright, and title pages.

- **Departmental format.** Bring your manuscript into conformity with any special departmental formatting guidelines.

- **Printing.** Run the print–edit–review cycle one final time on the entire manuscript, and set it in stone. Before printing the finished work, note that some departments require at least one copy on acid-free paper, although many brands of inexpensive laser-printer paper now meet acid-free specifications. After printing the copies for your committee and degree submission, go through each sheet to verify that the laser printer did its job correctly; after all that work and due diligence you will be disappointed if your bound copy in the university archives has six blank pages or, worse still, ten missing pages.

Throughout these concluding steps, operate in a deliberate, methodical manner. Slow down; exercise care and caution. Avoid introducing errors that were not there before and which you will not spot subsequently. It is all too easy to inadvertently tap the keyboard or brush it with a sheaf of papers, thereby entering rogue characters. Whenever you suspect you may have done so, click Undo Typing (<Ctrl> <Z>) and check where your cursor is sitting. I apologize for belaboring what may seem to be picky issues, and yet the details are every bit as crucial to your project's success as the big picture of your overarching thesis. Remember, attention to detail may not consciously impress busy professors who are evaluating a thesis or dissertation, but nothing will stick in their minds more, distracting them from the candidate's message, than silly mistakes and unforced errors. Soon after celebrating your successful—and well earned—defense, a feeling of anticlimax will settle in, which is perhaps as it should be, as you gear up for the consummate achievement of publishing your first article or monograph.

PUBLISHING AN ARTICLE OR MONOGRAPH

Providing you have an original thesis supported by innovative research and convincingly presented in a quality manuscript, there is no reason why you should not try to publish—and succeed in so doing—a peer-reviewed journal article before you defend your MA thesis or PhD dissertation. Doctoral candidates should aim to publish at least one article before their defense, although publishing more than two or three chapters may make a university press editor less inclined to consider a monograph. Set your sights on the top-ranked international journal in your field, and work your way down. Even though the submission–rejection process is time consuming, you will receive useful feedback along the way, and gain a sense of your manuscript's merit.

PEER REVIEW PROCESS

Top-ranked international journals—the only journals in which you should aim to publish your scholarship, because anything less only serves to devalue it—adhere to a rigorous peer review process. Having decided that your submission is worthy of further consideration, an editor will send your paper anonymously to two or three leading academics in your field, who will write detailed reports, also anonymously, including a recommendation to either publish the piece with limited changes, publish after a substantial rewrite and re-submission, or not publish at all.

Submission

By the time you are ready to publish an article, you will already be familiar with the leading journals in your field, although it is still worthwhile to browse your library's shelves to make the acquaintance of journals in peripheral fields and perhaps discover a new publication in your own field. It is always best to publish in your field's top journal, but also factor in backlog, suitability, and connections. Inquire from the journal's editor or on the scholarly grapevine whether there is a backlog; some journals have a wait time of two years but others can publish in the next edition. If your paper uses a particular methodology or speaks to a regional interest then you might consider a lower-ranked journal that matches your specialty. Similarly, when narrowing down a number of top contenders, favor the journal that recently published your dissertation advisor or which has an editorial board member who provided commentary for your last conference presentation.

Once you have selected the target for your first submission, look through the last few editions for hints on style and formatting, and check the submission requirements (some journals now carry this information only on their websites). Adhere to word limits—6,500 does not mean 7,300—and note that publication length can differ from submission length; having accepted an article, reviewers may ask the author to add content or develop a particular point. When converting a dissertation chapter to a journal article, be prepared to axe sentences, paragraphs, or even entire sections that are peripheral to the article's thesis, which will probably be a subset of or a variation on the dissertation's thesis. Précising the chapter to article length will be a useful exercise, focusing your attention on excessive evidence, and the perennial problem of falling in love with one's sources. Tailor your article's introductory paragraphs to the target journal's readership. Write a 150-word single-paragraph abstract that summarizes your topic, mentions your sources, and explains your thesis and its historiographical importance. Make your submission as professional as possible; on the Abstract page following the cover sheet, include this statement: "I confirm that this manuscript has not been published elsewhere and is not currently under consideration for publication in any other journal. If the manuscript is accepted, I agree to sign a contract for the transfer of copyright to the publisher." In addition to including it on the cover sheet, give the paper's title—but not your name—on the first page.

Additional considerations apply when preparing a monograph for submission, which William Germano covers in his comprehensive *Getting It Published*. Most fundamentally, you should recognize that few dissertations make it into print without a major rewrite. Dissertations inevitably become the product of the doctoral candidate's passion, with an admixture of the committee members' pet interests. They tend to contain theoretical, methodological, and historiographical sections bordering on treaties, moreover, for which a broader scholarly public would have little interest and less need. Left unrevised and unexpurgated, your manuscript will solicit comments from university press editors like, "I am afraid this study is too narrow for our press's catalogue." Try to decide, at the outset, to whom your work will best appeal—scholars, students, government agencies, history buffs—and tailor it accordingly. Soliciting opinions from colleagues, presenting sections of your work at conferences, and generally sitting on the manuscript for a few months can all be productive strategies. In my own case, the path to publication took twice as long as producing the dissertation itself, requiring the melding together of two chapters, the cutting of one chapter entirely, and the writing of a new introduction and conclusion, in addition to a raft of revisions to tone, voice, and content. When you are satisfied you have done all you can to knock the project into shape, submit it in conformity with the journal or press's submission requirements and wait.

Reviewers' Reports

Academia, as my advisor often remarked, alternates between spells of feverish activity and agonizingly long waits. Be patient but prepared to respond quickly with each turn of events, which hopefully will begin with a notification that the editor has sent your manuscript out for review, a process typically taking four to twelve weeks. Put aside your dreams that the two or three reviewers will wax lyrically about your brilliant scholarship, because when their reports arrive it will be all you can do not to abandon your scholarly career or stand in front of an express train. Take a deep breath and decode the editor's email. A comment like, "the reviewers are interested in publishing your article but feel that it needs work before they are able to accept it for publication," is actually cause for celebration not suicide, because the editor is saying that providing you make the necessary changes, his journal will publish your article. You will feel angry at the reviewers who say, "the writing is excessively clichéd," "there is insufficient evidence to support the argument," or "the argument's importance needs clarification," and embarrassed that there were three new monographs you failed to read, seven words you misspelled, and fourteen facts you stated incorrectly. But understand that the reviewers, however much they may pick holes in your exposition or disagree with your argument, are top scholars in your field, and they are making constructive—not destructive—comments designed to improve the quality of the published piece.

That said, there is nothing more demoralizing than an email from an editor declining publication, and reviewers' reports that are destructive. Yet as my own experience indicates, this does not mean you should give up and seek employment in a fast food restaurant. When I submitted my first book manuscript to a leading American university press, the editor was initially enthusiastic, but the two reviewers took personal offense to what they (incorrectly) believed my politics to be, accusing me of being an anti-Semitic Nazi propagandist and an intellectual failure who padded bibliographies, presented actors' lies as truths, argued to a gross double standard, and abdicated professional responsibility as a historian. Once I had accepted that the vicious—and unprofessional—character assassination was a product of the reviewers' own political biases, I sent my proposal to two dozen university presses, receiving six requests for the manuscript from eager editors, the first of which resulted in a book contract.

Revision and Pre-Press

Having digested the reviews, write an email to the editor explaining how you will be happy to rectify the problems raised by the reviewers. Sit on the email for at least a day to allow your blood pressure to stabilize, and read it again before sending; do not burn any bridges as the academic universe is surprisingly small. Reviewers' comments fall into three broad categories: First, grammatical, factual, and interpretational errors, all of which you should and will easily rectify. In the rare event that the reviewer is in error, corroborate your position with at least two other reliable sources and explain it with care and politeness to the editor. Second, problems—ranging from weaknesses to omissions—with your evidence and argumentation, and perhaps, too, with background and historiography. Again, you should, and will no doubt, fix all these problems. Although it will try your patience, do not resubmit without fully addressing the criticisms, because the editor has less patience than you do, and may respond with a final rejection. Instead, seek help from an independent reader, someone who has never seen the project before, perhaps a faculty member with whom you took a class, or a scholar you met at a conference. My first article submission, a piece on U.S. history to a European journal, lacked context for a non-American reader, which a scholar of British history whom I asked for advice quickly identified and helped me to address. Third, comments that you, the editor, and the reviewer tacitly understand to be optional, the kind of comments suggestive of an article the reviewer would like to have written based on your evidence. Incorporate as many of these optional changes as you see fit, but do not sell out your scholarship simply to please the reviewer. Deciding which issues are critical problems you must fix and which are optional enhancements is, of course, tricky, but remember that the editor's role is arbitration; provide a balanced commentary on the enhancements you have and have not made—and why—and ask the editor for guidance.

Shortly after you re-submit the revised manuscript, the editor will confirm (or otherwise) that it met the reviewers' concerns, and explain publication procedures and schedules. A copy editor will then email to you page proofs of the article, as it will appear on the printed page, typically as a PDF. Providing your submission was to the quality advocated in this guide, the copy editor will have made few changes, but be sure to not only review the edits carefully but also check the entire manuscript one more time, because errors can creep in during the editing and formatting process.

PROFESSIONAL ETHICS

Whether you are a third-year undergraduate or a departmental head, it is in your best interests to consider yourself a professional, and your chosen discipline as a profession. In the case of history, one of the strictest and most influential governing bodies is the American Historical Association, whose open-access website provides without charge the AHA's *Statement on Standards of Professional Conduct*, which all historians capable of reading English should study. In particular, note the sections on "Plagiarism" and "Reputation and Trust."

Padding and Plagiarism

Simply because your country's university system has created a publish-or-perish climate, or because your colleagues do so, is no excuse for padding your curriculum vitae with journal articles, chapters in edited collections, entries in compendia, and so forth that rehash arguments you previously made, based on research you conducted years earlier. Worse still, as happens too often in East Asia, avoid the temptation of copying the ideas of other scholars. Rather than succumb to the prevailing system, selling your scholarship short in the processes, become an advocate at your institution for the highest professional standards and a zero-tolerance policy toward plagiarism. Each time you convince a colleague to follow suit, you increase the chances of your institution becoming a leader in your field, recognized the world over for an excellence that will soon devolve onto your own work and reputation.

GRAMMAR AND STYLE ESSENTIALS

Ten Most Common Stylistic Problems
1. passive voice masks action.
2. multiple tenses: flipping from past to present tense.
3. confusion over that/which usage.
4. pronoun disagreement. [Congress met in session and they passed the act ✘] [. . . it passed the act ✔]
5. *however* misuse/overuse (instead, try *but, yet, although, still*).
6. lists omit comma before *and.* [red, white and blue ✘] [red, white, and blue ✔]
7. capitalization. [Spain's president said to President Bush ✔]
8. contractions and colloquialisms. [can't go wrong ✘]
9. centuries, and numbers less than 100, not spelled out. [the 20th century was 20 days old ✘]
10. misplaced footnote reference number; punctuation outside quote marks. [Bush called it an "Axis of Evil."⁴ ✔]

Opening Gambits
Instead of starting every other sentence with *The* or *In 1776*, scan back through the rough draft of each paragraph and invert the word order of selected sentences. [The Welsh dragoons, true to form, charged in with reckless abandon.] Revised: [True to form, the Welsh dragoons charged in with reckless abandon.] English has a wealth of introductory gambits, although be careful here, for words such as *nevertheless* are often better employed within a sentence rather than at the beginning. Some possibilities, with commas where typically applicable:

Yet | Besides, | Moreover, | Nevertheless, | Nonetheless, | In short, | In sum, | In addition, | In/by contrast, | Indeed, | Further, | Furthermore, | Though | Although | Still, | Hitherto, | Hereby, | Therefore | Thus | So | Increasingly | Additionally, | Meanwhile, | At the same time, | At this time, | Instead | In fact, | Insofar as | Whatever | Despite | Given that | Importantly, | Ultimately, | It is noteworthy that | Notwithstanding |

And | And yet, | But | are allowed in formal writing, only use them sparingly, and then for effect or emphasis. You make opening gambits such as *Moreover, Furthermore,* and *Indeed* sound less pedantic when you embed them within a sentence, and you should never use the following to open a sentence:

however, | for example, | for instance, | also |

Instead, embed them in the sentence. [Patton had already decided, however, to . . . ✔] [On the morning of the sixteenth, for instance, Patton . . ." ✔] Still, work at reducing instances of *for instance, such as,* and especially *for example* because they cost you two words and are frequently moot. After all, if you are including evidence then it is automatically an example. Even advanced writers sometimes use *however* when they really mean *but, yet, although,* or *though.* And *however* is one of those words that stops your reader cold, so reserve it for special occasions. Words like *clearly* do not belong in introductions, and do limit their use in body paragraphs; providing that your evidence selection and forensic skills adequately support your thesis, then things may well be clear by the time you reach your conclusion. Saying that something is clear does not make it so.

Standard Constructions

English has tried and tested phrasial patterns that simply sound right, so stick with them.

If *X* then *Y.* (Note, there is no intervening comma.)

Not only *X* but also *Y.* (Similarly, no intervening comma.)

This *X* but not that *Y.*

On the one hand, *X.* On the other hand, *Y.*

First, . . . Second, . . . Third, . . . [or] Finally, . . .

Commas

On the one hand, grammatical rules govern many aspects of comma usage, while on the other hand, with advanced style comes longer sentences and the need for commas to enhance readability. Ultimately, as *Chicago* says, "Effective use of the comma involves good judgement, with ease of reading the end in view." So, below, I list some of the rules, but I admit to overusing—and occasionally misusing—the comma in my own writing.

- Always include a comma after the penultimate item in a series. [American flags are red, white, and blue. ✓] [Are you cold, hungry, or thirsty? ✓]

- Set off adverbial phrases that lie between the subject and the verb with commas. [Cardinal Gomá, on receiving the telegram, sat down and wrote a lengthy reply. ✓]

- A comma is not strictly necessary after short introductory adverbial phrases of less than four words. [After returning home Cardinal Gomá drafted his reply. ✓]

- Historians, though, commonly include one after an introductory date. [In May 1930, Gomá wrote a pastoral letter. ✓]

- Set off introductory participle phrases with a comma, unless followed by a verb. [Charging into battle, Alexander set a noble example. ✓] [Charging into battle was Alexander himself. ✓]

- Avoid commas where they might limit or restrict meaning. [Cardinal Gomá's pastoral letter, *Grave Hours,* was a rhetorical masterpiece.] Implies he wrote only one pastoral. [Cardinal Gomá's pastoral letter *Grave Hours* was a rhetorical masterpiece.] In fact, he wrote many.

- Use commas to set off parenthetical elements; use em-dashes for independent clauses. [Maier's book, for the most part, is hard to follow. ✓] [Maier's book—as with so many other French translations—is hard to follow. ✓]

Dashes, Spacing

For compound words—when they are adjectives but not nouns—as in "high-fidelity sound system," or "nineteenth-century wartime experiences," use a plain dash, or hyphen. Note the distinction between adjectives and nouns. [Tom carried machine-gun bullets, Dick carried the machine gun. ✓] Following *Chicago*'s guidance, when readability is an issue I err on the side of hyphenating compounds.

En-dash. For number and date ranges, like "1914–18," "pp. 519–605," or "July–August 1942," use an en-dash (hold down <Ctrl> while pressing <-> on the numeric keypad). If you want to say *from* then you do not use the en-dash as well; in other words, "from July to August," never, "from July–August." Wars and treaties between parties also use en-dashes not hyphens. [Russo–Japanese War; Rome–Berlin Axis; Adams–Onís Treaty. ✓]

Em-dash. To set off independent clauses—as here—use the em-dash (hold down <Ctrl> and <Alt> while pressing <->).[1] As your sentences become longer and more complex, practice using pairs of em-dashes. Sample thesis statement using em-dashes to set off a paper's five main points: [This paper will argue—through a discussion of Thomas More's views on property ownership, religious tolerance, seditious behavior, crime and punishment, and meritocracy—that *Utopia* was both a warning of impending revolution and a manual for social control.]

In contradistinction to *Chicago*, I advocate **double-spacing** between sentences (though not after colons); set MS-Word to check for this, and double-space after each period consistently throughout your manuscript. An extra space after a sentence is esthetically pleasing, improves readability, and avoids confusion when a sentence ends or begins with an abbreviation or initial. Similarly, for multi-initial personal names, I do not insert a space between the initials. Remove periods from abbreviated entities, unless it creates confusion. [D.F. Smith was U.S. ambassador to the UN. ✓]

Dates, Numbers

Most American historians now use the *Chicago* recommended day-month-year format, which does not require any intervening commas. [Cardinal Gomá went to Toledo on 5 November 1936. Three days later, on 8 November, he returned to Pamplona. Two days after that, on the tenth, he met with his secretary. ✓]

---

1. With laptops, you first need to hold down the function key that activates your numeric keys; this is a tad awkward but, with practice, soon becomes automatic. (MS-Word will also generate this automatically if you type: character, space, dash, space, character, space, but this method takes several extra key strokes and you have to go back and delete out the two unwanted spaces.) On Apples: <Apple> <Minus> = en-dash; <Apple> <Alt> <Minus> = em-dash. Note that MS-Word lets you customize your own keyboard shortcuts (shortcut keys).

This modern format scans better and saves commas.

MS-Word wants to superscript ordinals [the 115th edition of *Time* ✖]; stop it from doing this by leaving a space and then back-spacing [the 115th edition ✓], or, better still, by turning off the option in Auto-Correct. Only rarely, though, will you find yourself in this situation, for you should always spell out numbers of ninety-nine or lower.

Decades are not possessive, so write "the 1930s" and never "the 1930's." (Popular in the 1950s and 1960s, this latter format has been anachronistic ever since.) Centuries, when adjectives, are hyphenated, and when nouns, are un-hyphenated. [Nineteenth-century warfare was different from war in the twentieth century. ✓] There are, of course, exceptions to rules, such as, percentages, weapon systems, and military units. [Casualties were 27 percent after the 88s of the 5th Panzer Division opened fire. ✓]

When giving page ranges, do not abbreviate numbers less than 100 [pp. 77–93]; use all digits for multiples of 100 [pp. 200–204], and the last digit for the first nine numbers in a century [pp. 301–7]; abbreviate other numbers using two digits, as required [pp. 344–51, 596–602, 613–20]. Notice the space after a *p.* or *pp.*

Orphaned Participle (Gerund) Clauses

To make your writing more interesting, practice opening the occasional sentence with a participle phrase. But the phrase must modify the sentence's grammatical subject. [Living in an increasingly pluralistic society, ethnic diversity rather than varied political ideology had become the arbiter of successful policy. ✖] Here, ethnic diversity, which is the subject, cannot live in a pluralistic society; people not concepts live in a society.

That/Which Usage

Use *that* for restrictive clauses and *which* for non-restrictive clauses, with the latter set off by a pair of commas. In other words, if the sentence would not make sense were the clause removed then use *that*, but if you could omit the clause without crippling the sentence then use *which*. [Boston has a climate that chills you to the bone.] [Boston, which is a windy city, is my home.] In these two examples, [Boston has a climate.] hardly makes sense, but [Boston is my home.] is a complete sentence.

Fractured English

If you are prone to the problem of fractured sentences then first, to impress on yourself the nature of the beast, try this: read your work aloud and see how it sounds; better still, ask a friend to read it back to you. Always be careful with carry-overs, stand-ins, and pronouns (this, their, he/him, it, its); make clear to whom or to what you are referring. Once you have more than one actor (voice) in a paragraph, knowing who is doing/saying what to whom becomes especially problematic, as when you have three persons of the same gender. Avoid confusion by using actors' names, even at the risk of repetition or appearing excessively precise. While synonyms (Roosevelt; the president; FDR; the man in the Oval Office) may alleviate repetition, avoid excessive journalese; your reader will much prefer repetition to bewilderment. If in any doubt then write explicitly not implicitly.

Pronoun Disagreement

Even advanced writers struggle with pronoun agreement. One way to minimize the problem is to use proper nouns, and, especially, by plugging in real, live historical actors instead of groups and nations. [In 1898, the United States invaded Cuba, but the Teller Amendment prohibited them from annexing the island. ✗] Changing *them* to *it* would fix the bad grammar, as would changing *the United States* to *Americans*, which also saves two precious words. But by specifying the invaders, you could implicate, say, U.S. forces, Gen. William R. Shafter's troops, Jingoes, or even Theodore Roosevelt's Rough Riders.

Down-Style, Naming

Trends are toward less capitalization, a "parsimonious use of capitals" that *Chicago* calls "down" style; some historians of religion are now writing, "the Catholic church." Uppercase titles only when directly preceding a name. "The president of Argentina met

President George W. Bush." "During the Civil War, most south-
erners fought for the South." Again, consistency is the rule. If you
are going to uppercase Blacks then do so throughout. On first
mentioning a personage, give full name and any official title:
President Richard M. Nixon, Field Marshal Bernard Law
Montgomery, Rep. John W. McCormack (D-MA), Cardinal
Francis Spellman, Prime Minister Kim Il-sung. But in subsequent
paragraphs, just give family name: Nixon, Montgomery,
McCormack, Spellman, Kim. Handle terms and organizations
that you will use more than once like this: "Congress of Industrial
Organizations (CIO) . . ." When used as a noun, spell out "the
United States" but abbreviate when used as an adjective: "Nixon
understood U.S. foreign policy to mean . . ." Note: while "the
United States" is a singular noun, its possessive breaks the rule: "in
the United States' opinion, Vietnam was . . ." but you can avoid
this awkward construction by plugging in people: "in policymakers' opinions, Vietnam was . . ."

Capitalization and Style—Examples from a U.S. Perspective

the Western Hemisphere	the East Coast
the South	southern Baptists
redcoats	Britons
laissez-faire	realpolitik
the colonial period	the Progressive Era
the Jazz Age	the Roaring Twenties
the Industrial Revolution	the New Deal
World War II	the Cold War
the Fourth of July	September 11 or 9/11
the Monroe Doctrine	the doctrine
USS *Maine*	the U.S. Constitution
Chiang Kai-shek	Mao Zedong
Guomindang	Chinese Communist Party
art deco	modernism
postmodernism	church and state
the State Department	the Secretary of State
the Senate	the senators

the United States Army	the army
the Communist Party	the communists
the Right	the right wing
the West	Western world (as cultural term)

Anathemous Words and Phrases

Reserve words like *saw* and *viewed* for people; never say, "the new day witnessed much bloodshed," or "America frowned on China's policy," because days are blind and countries are eyebrow-less chunks of land; plug in actors and watch your prose come alive. Banish euphemisms; instead of "Reagan passed on," say simply "Reagan died." Do not drop prepositions [the student graduated college ✗] [the student graduated from college ✓]. Say either "during the time" or "during the period" but never "during the time period," which would be redundant.

banish:	use instead:	banish:	use instead:
amidst	amid	and more	[TV-speak]
amongst	among	as of yet	yet
dove	dived	at the present time	now
etc., i.e.,	[be explicit]	at the time that	when
ongoing	continuing	due to the fact that	because
pled	pleaded	firstly, secondly	first, second
prior to	before	got, gotten	[ugly; reword]
spark	incite	had had; that that	[rephrase]
spilt	spilled	one of the methods	one method
towards	toward	plus [he was . . .]	and [he was]
utilize	use	somewhere	[often superfluous]

American vs. British English

It is easy to pick up bad habits when reading books printed some time ago or outside the United States. In British English, quotations go between single marks, while quotations-within-quotations are in double marks; punctuation goes outside the quote marks; the penultimate item in a series has no separating comma; that and which are interchangeable. British English looks like this: 'Be sure to buy parsnips, turnips and Swedes', she shouted after him, 'and a bag of those "Spanish" onions'.

TIPS FOR EAST ASIAN WRITERS

Adopt the grammar and style of American rather than British English, including the simpler and more logical American spelling, and pay particular attention to the following points:

- Do not use the so-called royal, Victorian, or perhaps Mongol *we*. [McNeill's argument is insightful, although we should not consider his three variations as separate parts. ✗] Either use the first person plural or recast the sentence to remove the opinionated pronoun. [McNeill's argument is insightful, although I do not consider his three variations as separate parts. ✓] [McNeill's argument is insightful, although his three variations hardly constitute separate parts. ✓]
- Italicize published works (but not the titles of journal articles).
- Minimize uppercasing—practice down-style.
- *That* and *which* are not interchangeable as in British English.
- Ensure that punctuation is inside quotation marks, and footnote reference numbers are outside the marks.
- Triple check that you have transcribed quotations verbatim from the original source.
- be careful, particularly in footnotes, to only use Asian fonts (FangSong, SimSun) for Chinese characters.

Definite Article

Many East Asian writers misplace *the* when writing English. Experience develops a natural sense of which nouns require a *the*, but there are rules to make the learning process less of a hit-or-miss affair. Use the definite article *the* in front of singular or plural nouns referring to a specific member of a group. [The boy ran across the road. ✓] Use an indefinite article *a* or *an* in front of a singular noun referring to any member of a group. [A boy ran across a road. ✓] Do not use an article—the zero article—in front of an indefinite plural. [Boys like running across roads. ✓] Notice, too, that there is no article in front of proper nouns. [David ran across Fulham Road. ✓] Naturally, there are exceptions, as when adjectives behave like proper nouns, but best practice is to memorize the rule and just learn the exceptions as you encounter them. [David called it Great Britain but Susan called it the United Kingdom. ✓]

MS-WORD 2010 SETTINGS

Measurements setting: inches.

1-Body Text   To create a new style for your body paragraphs, on Word's menu bar, click: Home—Styles—(click arrow on right)—New Style (bottom left); {Name: 1-Body Text}, {Style Type: Paragraph}, {Style based on: No Style}, {Style for following paragraph: 1-Body Text}. Format—Font—{Font: Times New Roman}, {Size: 12 pt}—Okay; Paragraph—Indents and Spacing—{Alignment: Left}, {Before: 0 pt}, {After: 0 pt}, {Indentation Left: 0.5 in}, {Indentation Right: 0.5 in}, {Line Spacing: Exactly}, {At: 28 pt}, {Special: First Line}, {By: 0.38 in}—Okay.

2-Subhead   Home—Styles—New Style (bottom left); {Name: 2-Subhead}, {Style Type: Paragraph}, {Style based on: No Style}, {Style for following paragraph: 1-Body Text}. Format—Font—{Font: Times New Roman}, {Font Style: Bold}, {Size: 12 pt}—Okay; Paragraph—Indents and Spacing—{Outline Level: Level 1}, {Alignment: Left}, {Before: 16 pt}, {After: 0 pt}, {Indentation Left: 0.5 in}, {Indentation Right: 0.5 in}, {Line Spacing: Exactly}, {At: 15 pt}—Line and Page Breaks—{Keep with next: ☑}—Okay.

3-Chapter Heading   Home—Styles—New Style (bottom left); {Name: 3-Chapter Heading}, {Style Type: Paragraph}, {Style based on: No Style}, {Style for following paragraph: 1-Body Text}. Format—Font—{Font: Times New Roman}, {Font Style: Bold}, {Size: 13 pt}, {Effects: ☑ All caps}—Okay; Paragraph—Indents and Spacing—{Outline Level: Level 1}, {Alignment: Left}, {Before: 0 pt}, {After: 6 pt}, {Indentation Left: 0.5 in}, {Indentation Right: 0.5 in}, {Line Spacing: Exactly}, {At: 20 pt}—Line and Page Breaks—{Keep with next: ☑}—Okay.

Footnote Text   Home—Styles (click arrow)—Footnote Text—Modify [highlight, then click Down-Arrow]—

Format—Font—{Font: Times New Roman}, {Size: 10 pt}. Paragraph—Indents and Spacing—{Alignment: Left}, {Before: 2 pt}, {After: 2 pt}, {Indentation Left: 0.5 in}, {Indentation Right: 0.5 in}, {Line Spacing: Exactly}, {At: 16 pt}, {Special: First Line}, {By: 0.38 in}.

Footnote Separator, Continuation Separator, Continuation Notice   View—Footnotes—[click the Listbox at the top left of the footnote area]—Footnote Separator—[highlight the separator]—Format—Paragraph—Indents and Spacing—{Left: 0.5 in}. (Repeat for Continuation Separator, and Notice.)

Page Layout   Page Setup (arrow on right)—Margins—{Top: 1.0 in}, {Bottom: 0.8 in}, {Left: 0.5 in}, {Right: 0.5 in}, {Gutter: 0.0 in}; Layout—{Header: 0.6 in}, {Footer: 0.0 in}.

Page Number   View (Print Layout)—place cursor at top of page and double-click—Page Number—Top of Page Number—Plain Number 3.

Grammar   Word Options—Proofing—Grammar & Style—Settings—{Comma Required: always}, {Punctuation Required: Inside}, {Spaces Required: 2}, {All Grammar and Style checkboxes: ☑}.

AutoCorrect   Word Options—Proofing—AutoCorrect Options—AutoFormat As You Type—Replace as You Type—{☑ Straight Quotes with Smart Quotes} but {☐ Ordinals (1st) with superscript]. Experiment with other options.

Important note: do not use Word's Double Space setting because a strange software bug will invariably carry your footnotes over to the following page; instead, set {Line Spacing: Exactly}, {At: 28 pt}, as shown in 1-Body Text. Also note: if you are inserting a picture then you must set {Line Spacing: At least} for that particular paragraph, otherwise only one line's worth of the picture will be visible.

Document Map: In addition to presetting 3-Chapter Heading and 2-Subhead at Levels 1 and 2 respectively, as shown on the prior page, you can customize the level for particular text, paragraphs, or headings by switching to Outline view and then clicking the Outlining tab.

Managing your Normal.dot template: Word Options—Add Ins—Manage—Templates—Organizer; this pops up a split pane, with Normal styles on the right and the styles that exist in your current document on the left. Now you can overwrite any Normal style with your document's modified style, and vice versa.

RHETORICAL CONSTRUCTS

acronym   use of a group of letters to represent a word or phrase in shortened form ("UN").

alliteration   the repetition of an initial letter or first sound of several words ("wicked witch of the west").

anachronism   an error of chronology; an event out of time or order.

antinomy   the irreconcilability of seemingly necessary inferences or conclusions (as in a paradox).

aphorism   a maxim.

banality   a commonplace, overused, or trivialized phrase.

bon mot   literally, *good word*; a witticism, a wisecrack.

casuistry   subtly deceptive argumentation, along moral or ethical lines, often through the application or extension of basic principles.

catch-22   an inescapable dilemma, typically caused by excessive regulations or illogical conditions.

cliché   a stereotyped, hackneyed expression.

counterpoint   the juxtaposition of contrapuntal or oppositional themes.

cynicism   contempt or criticism for virtues and generous sentiments of others.

dichotomy   a division into two parts or moieties; oppositional concepts, ideas, constructs.

epigram   a pithy, caustic, or thought-provoking saying or short poem.

epithet   a phrase used adjectivally; an evocative nickname.

euphemism   the substitution of an inoffensive term for one with unpleasant associations.

homonym   two words that are pronounced or spelled the same but have different meanings.

hyperbole   inordinate exaggeration, perhaps calculatedly so.

hypocrisy extreme insincerity; dissimulation.

idiom an expression not readily analyzable from its grammatical or linguistic construction.

incongruity an unsuitable or inharmonious statement.

irony a statement/situation that signifies the opposite of what it means or implies.

litotes an exaggerated or ironic understatement ("it was a matter of no little importance").

macaronic a medley of foreign words, either real or imaginary.

malapropism a verbal blunder or inappropriate word usage.

metaphor a word or phrase denoting one kind of idea/thing in place of another.

metonym a figurative expression or attribute standing in for another concept or thing, such as *laurels* for *honor* or *Brussels* for *the capital of the European Union*.

neologism coining a new word; borrowing a word from another language.

onomatopoeia imitation of natural sounds by words ("hiss," "crack").

oxymoron combination of contradictory words ("he endured a living death").

paradox a statement that appears contradictory yet is true in fact; a weighty, solvable riddle.

paralogism admittedly false knowledge; refers to the unknown.

patronymic deriving one's name from a male ancestor; one's name is the same as a famous person in a similar calling.

pleonasm the use of needless words ("chain mail" instead of simply "mail").

sarcasm the practice of keen irony; contemptuous or taunting language.

semiotics study of signs and symbols, and their relationship to ideas (adj. semiotic).

simile   comparison by means of *like* or *as* between two kinds of ideas/things.

sobriquet   a nickname; a fanciful or humorous name.

synecdoche   a part standing in for a whole, or vice versa (as in, a saddle for a horse, or a hearth for a house).

synonyms   words with common meanings.

tautologism   needlessly repetitive statements; rhetorical self-truths ("this history internationalizes international relations").

trope   the figurative use of a word; something standing in for something else.

truism   a platitude, or self-evident truth.

venality   a base or sordid expression.

USEFUL—AND MISUSED—WORDS   learn for GRE

abstruse	hard to understand.
accidie	mental or spiritual torpor; sloth.
anathema	a ban or curse; something detested.
anodyne	soothing; relieves pain.
anomie	society's values are irrelevant (absent).
aphorism	maxim.
apodictic	clearly demonstrable.
appetence	tendency; instinct.
apposite	appropriate.
asperity	harshness, severity.
assiduous	hard working.
aver	claim to be true.
bathos	from lofty to banal discourse.
credulous	easily deceived.
cupidity	avarice; inordinate wish for possession.
demotic	of the people (not aristocratic); popular.
diachronic	persisting, existing through time.
didactic	nature of teaching; morally instructive.
disabuse	correct a fallacy, clarify.
dissemble	pretend, simulate.
dissipation	intemperance.
efficacy	power to produce the desired effect.
encomium	formal expression of praise.
enervation	lack of energy.
entrepôt	trading port, post; market.
epigraphy	study of inscriptions, epitaphs.
equable	steady, uniform.
estimable	worthy of esteem and admiration.
excoriation	act of condemning with harsh words.
exculpate	to free from blame or guilt.
exegesis	explanation of a literary work.
exigent	urgent, requiring immediate attention.
extirpate	root out, destroy.
gainsay	contradict or oppose.

gnomic	dealing in maxims.
gnostic	possessing knowledge, insight.
hagiography	reverential biography; study of saints' lives.
holistic	natural trend toward organized synthesis.
hermeneutics	interpretation of texts, esp. Biblical ones.
impecunious	having no money; perpetually poor.
inchoate	not fully developed or formulated.
incommensurable	lacking a standard of comparison.
ineluctable	inescapable.
inimical	unfriendly, hostile; adverse, difficult.
insouciance	careless unconcern; indifference.
involution	entanglement; rhetorical complexity.
irenic	conciliatory.
irredentist	advocating reunion with the mother country.
laconic	concise, sparing with words.
limn	to outline in detail; to delineate.
litotes	exaggerated understatement.
lugubrious	mournful; exaggeratedly sad, doleful.
macaronic	medley of words from different languages.
manqué	defective; inadequate.
meme	inheritable cultural characteristic.
mendacious	addicted to lying; deceitful.
minatory	menacing, threatening.
misanthrope	one who hates or distrusts all people.
moot	subject to discussion; unimportant.
neologism	new word, new meaning for old word.
noisome	putrid, noxious.
novum	implies a new order or paradigm.
ochlocracy	mob rule; government by populace.
paean	joyous expression of gratitude.
paleography	science of deciphering ancient writing.
panegyric	formal public eulogy (written or spoken).
particularism	fidelity to interests of one's state, party.
pedantic	academic, bookish.
peripatetic	always on the go.
perspicacity	keenness of perception.

philology	study of written records, linguistics.
picayune	worthless, petty, trifling.
probity	goodness, integrity.
prodigality	wastefulness.
prolixity	rambling, verbose quality.
propitiating	conciliatory, mollifying.
proscribe	denounce; prohibit; interdict.
protean	readily assuming different forms, changing.
putative	supposed, reported, reputed.
quiescent	state of rest or inactivity.
quotidian	occurring every day; commonplace.
recidivism	backsliding into a former (bad) state.
recondite	profound, deep, abstruse.
refractory	stubbornly resisting control or authority.
restive	restless; impatient.
salutary	restorative, healthful.
sectary	dissenter, nonconformist; a sectarian.
sedulous	diligent, industrious.
semiotics	study of symbols and their meaning.
sidereal	relating to the stars or constellations.
sphragistics	study of signet rings, engraved seals.
sublime	grand; solemn.
swidden	slash-and-burn agriculture.
sybaritic	proclivity to luxury; voluptuous.
synchronic	a study at a fixed point, rather than over time.
tendentious	having a purposed aim.
teleology	philosophy of purposive causation.
trenchant	caustic and incisive.
turpitude	depravity, wickedness.
tyro	novice, amateur.
unalloyed	unqualified, pure.
urbanity	sophistication, suaveness, and polish.
veracious	truthful, earnest.
viscid	sticky.
vitiate	pollute, impair.
vituperative	verbally abusive, insulting.

Ambiguous Words and Phrases

beg the question means to assume the validity of one's argument; it does not mean to pose or prompt a question.

biannual, semiannual write: "twice a year" (biennial, "every two years"; biweekly, "every two weeks"; semiweekly, "twice a week").

bring, take for actions directed toward the observer use *bring*, and away use *take*. He took his laptop to the archive and brought files back.

cull can mean to choose from a group (to keep) as well as to select from a group (to discard).

emigrate, immigrate viewpoint dependant. In a study about nineteenth-century Ireland: "conditions became so dire that Colleen O'Reilly decided to emigrate to America." But in a study on nineteenth-century America: "Colleen O'Reilly was one of nine hundred new immigrants who disembarked at the Port of New York that day."

moot a moot question is an arguable point, but a moot issue is an irrelevancy.

sanction as a verb, means permit, but as a noun, either penalty or approval.

table a motion Westminster or Brussels: put a motion on the table for discussion. Capitol Hill: remove the motion from the table and shelve it.

BIBLIOGRAPHY

Burke, Peter. *Eyewitnessing: The Uses of Images as Historical Evidence.* Ithaca, NY: Cornell University Press, 2007. Also in Chinese, Yang Yu, trans. Beijing: Peking University Press, 2008.

Chapman, James. *Cinemas of the World: Film and Society, from 1895 to the Present.* London: Reaktion, 2003.

The Chicago Manual of Style. 16th edition. Chicago: University of Chicago Press, 2010.

Germano, William. *Getting It Published: A Guide for Scholars and Anyone Else Serious about Serious Books.* Chicago: University of Chicago Press, 2008.

Hoffer, Peter Charles. *Past Imperfect: Facts, Fictions, Fraud—American History from Bancroft and Parkman to Ambrose, Bellesiles, Ellis, and Goodman.* New York: Public Affairs, 2007.

Kingery, W. David, ed. *Learning from Things: Method and Theory of Material Culture Studies.* Washington, DC: Smithsonian Institution Press, 1996.

Marius, Richard. *A Short Guide to Writing About History.* 3rd edition. New York: Longman, 1999.

New Oxford Dictionary for Writers and Editors: The Essential A–Z Guide to the Written Word. Oxford: Oxford University Press, 2005.

Orwell, George. "Politics and the English Language." *Horizon,* 13:76 (April 1946), pp. 252–65. Commonly available on the web.

Oxford English Reference Dictionary. Judy Pearsall and Bill Trumble, eds. Oxford: Oxford University Press, 2003.

Riffe, Daniel, Stephen Lacy, and Frederick G. Fico. *Analyzing Media Messages: Using Quantitative Content Analysis in Research.* Mahwah, NJ: Lawrence Erlbaum Associates, 1998.

Ritchie, Donald A. *Doing Oral History: A Practical Guide.* New

York: Oxford University Press, 2003.

Schlereth, Thomas J., ed. *Material Culture Studies in America.* Nashville, TN: American Association for State and Local History, 1982.

Siegal, Allan M., and William G. Connolly. *The New York Times Manual of Style and Usage.* New York: Three Rivers Press, 1999.

Strunk, William, Jr., and E.B. White. *The Elements of Style.* 4th edition. New York: Longman Publishers, 2000.

ABBREVIATIONS

Military Abbreviations

Adm. Admiral.

Capt. Captain.

Cmdr. Commodore, Commander.

Lt. Lieutenant.

Maj. Gen. Major General.

Sgt. Sergeant.

Footnote and Bibliography Abbreviations and Terms

b. box [box, hereafter b.].

c. carton [carton, hereafter c.].

ca. (circa), about, approximately; ca. 1934 indicates that the date is an estimate.

chap. chaps. one chapter, several chapters.

Cong. Congress.

ed. eds. one editor, several editors.

esp. especially.

et al. (*et alia*, and others) for four or more authors, give the first author's name in full, followed by et al.

f. ff. one folder, several folders, [folder, hereafter, f.].

fn. footnote.

ibid. (*ibidem*, from the same source) same source as prior footnote.

id. (*idem*, from the same) same author as prior footnote.

min. minute or minutes; for runtime of movies.

n. nn. footnote, footnotes.

n.d. no date.

no. number.

n.p. no place, or no publisher, meaning the information is absent.

passim (here and there) for scattered references over a range of pages.

sess. session.

trans. translator.
U.S. GPO   U.S. Government Printing Office.
vol. vols.   one volume, several volumes.

In Text

sic   (thus) to denote text copied verbatim from the original that
is archaic or erroneous; to differentiate [*sic*] from the par-
ent quotation, set it in italics inside square brackets, as here.

EXAMPLES

Thesis Statement: Journal Article, Donggil Kim, 2010

It seems credible therefore, that Stalin's approval of Kim Il-sung's plan in January 1950 coincided with his understanding of a shift in the Soviet Union's national interests, prompting the question: why did Stalin suddenly change his attitude and agree with Kim's request to attack the South? What prompted his strategic U-turn? What occurred between December 1949 and January 1950 to change Stalin's position about war on the Korean Peninsula? This article's purpose, then, is first, to examine the changes that had occurred in the triangular relationship between America, China, and the USSR, and second, to determine which of these changes prompted Stalin's decision in late January 1950 to attack South Korea. Finally, through an analysis of recently uncovered Soviet documents, this paper shows how the Korean War figured into Stalin's evolving global security strategy, suggesting a new framework for viewing the outbreak of the Korean War.

I believe that Stalin's sudden decision to start a war in Korea needs explanation in the context of his overall global security strategy, and I propose that three interconnected factors combined to force him to modify his strategy on the Korean peninsula: First, there were important changes in the international environment, specifically in the U.S.–Sino–Soviet triangular relationship between December 1949 and January 1950. Second, there was Stalin's need to modify his existing security strategy in light of the Sino–Soviet negotiations in January 1950. Third, there were attempts by the capitalist camp to engage China, driving a wedge into Sino–Soviet relations, and exacerbating Stalin's mistrust of Mao. After reviewing prevailing explanations of the war, I will argue that these three factors combined to cause Stalin to approve Kim's request to attack the South, thereby launching the Korean War at the end of January 1950.[2]

---

2. Donggil Kim, "Stalin's Korean U-Turn: The USSR's Evolving Security Strategy and the Origins of the Korean War," draft manuscript, March 2010;

_____

These are the last two of six introductory paragraphs for a model journal article. In the penultimate paragraph, Kim briefly summarizes his introductory observations and issues; he then re-states the problem that his research has identified in the form of a question (actually a series of questions for emphasis). After out-lining the article's agenda, and alluding to his use of new sources and hence the article's importance, he points to a big-picture his-toriographical question that his case study addresses. In the last paragraph, Kim presents his thesis, which he frames in the context of the bigger picture, and explicitly states his three main points. He completes the road map by mentioning that the paper's first section will cover relevant historiography and finally restates his thesis for extra clarity.

Thesis Statement: Journal Article, Michael Chapman, 2006

After describing Sedgwick's seminal tour of Nationalist Spain with his friend W. Cameron Forbes, and discussing a selection of the *Atlantic*'s libertarian essayists, this article documents Sedgwick's activism for State Department recognition of Franco and his work-ing association with Kelly. It highlights the Great Debate's polar-ized red–fascist rhetoric, which backed liberal progressives into the conservatives' corner as well as laying the discursive groundwork for 1950s McCarthyism. It argues that Forbes and Sedgwick were not interested in Franco per se, but promoted his cause because they sought to demonstrate the danger that international commu-nism posed to American national identity during a period of un-precedented insecurity. Michael H. Hunt has observed that cli-mactic moments in the gradual and highly contested process of national-identity formation can arise when elites—often those with the strongest sense of national identity—respond to a foreign affairs crisis, yet their historically rooted patriotism may limit the scope and appropriateness of their responses. This article suggests that its actors mentally mapped Spain onto the United States, to

_____

Kim is associate professor of history at Peking University.

contrast the immoral and anarchic Other of encroaching foreign Marxism with the civilizing order of traditional American core values. Like later Cold Warriors, Franco lobbyists confronted the paradox of the necessary enemy, for while international communism represented the ultimate danger, continually fighting it provided the perfect justification for national security.[3]

I begin this concluding paragraph of a five-paragraph introduction with a road map, suggesting in the process that the article will document something for the first time. I provide a clear thesis statement, which I then frame in a bigger-picture concern, as identified by another historian. And I close by suggesting that my case study has relevance to—and perhaps its actors contributed toward—an important historical period. This paragraph took longer to write than I care to admit, its constructions being deliberate rather then happenstance. There is a planned progression—*describing, discussing, documents, argues, suggests*—and the *ah-dee-ess* alliterative/rhythmic phrasing in the first sentence was intentional. [After describing Sedgwick's . . . and discussing a selection . . . article documents Sedgwick's . . .] Note how I give names in full for Forbes and Hunt, but not for Sedgwick, Franco, or Kelly, as I introduced them in prior paragraphs; my original manuscript had "Historian Michael H. Hunt," which in this version I edited out to save words, although "has observes" suggests that Hunt is a contemporary scholar.

Textual Immersion: Walter LaFeber, 2008

Howard warned that the worst policy would be to invade sovereign Islamic nations, then call it a "war" against terrorism. Terrorists, he believed, should not be "dignified with the status of [country-based] belligerents: they were criminals" and should not be given "a status and dignity that they seek and that they do not deserve." He urged Bush to avoid a "catharsis"; that is, he should

---

3. Michael E. Chapman, "Pro-Franco Anti-Communism: Ellery Sedgwick and the *Atlantic Monthly*," *Journal of Contemporary History*, 41:4 (October 2006), pp. 641–62.

not try to avenge the 9/11 attacks with spectacular military actions. Such wars against Islamic nations would alienate even those Muslims who now despised al Qaeda. And to attack Iraq would resemble "the drunk who lost his watch in a dark alley but looked for it under a lamppost because there was more light there." Al Qaeda, Howard wrote, was not in Iraq, but did exist in many other countries. Bush should cooperate with other intelligence agencies, seize and break up the terrorist networks, then either kill the terrorists or bring them before the courts. To invade Islamic nations could turn those nations into breeding grounds for terrorists, while "eroding the moral authority" of the United States as it killed innocent civilians in the attack. Such an invasion would resemble "trying to eradicate cancer cells with a blowtorch." Vital areas (Turkey, Egypt, Pakistan) could be consumed in the flames, while the cancer's cause, Osama bin Laden, could escape and "cannot lose."[4]

This paragraph from the final chapter of a new edition of a book that first appeared in 1967, illustrates the modern trend toward textual immersion. LaFeber extracts key words [war, catharsis] and memorable phrases [the drunk who lost his watch] [eradicate cancer cells with a blowtorch] and embeds them in his own paraphrasing—"kill the terrorists or bring them before the courts" versus, "hunted down and brought before an international court" in the original—to make sense of what was a rather opaque speech. To ensure the reader understands that the voice is Howard's and not his own, notice how LaFeber posits Howard as doer on four occasions [Howard warned; he believed; he urged; Howard wrote]. For the most part, LaFeber is true to his source, although he does rather put words into Howard's mouth with his phrase, "To invade Islamic nations could turn those nations into breeding grounds for terrorists," for the closest Howard came to making such an assertion was in the next paragraph, with "[Images on television of] Western military action will strengthen the hatred and

4. Walter LaFeber, *America, Russia, and the Cold War, 1945–2006* (Boston, MA: McGraw-Hill, 2008), p. 418.

recruit for the ranks of the terrorists." A truer paraphrase would have been something like, "To invade Islamic nations would only strengthen local hatreds of Americans while increasing the supply of eager recruits to the terrorists' ranks."[5]

Textual Immersion: Seth Jacobs, 2010

Parsons's arrogance and narrow-mindedness might have been less damaging to U.S. policy had his fellow administrators in Vientiane seen matters differently, but the record left by the embassy, USOM, USIS, and other major American organizations indicates that the ambassador's views were, for the most part, shared by those officials whose authority approached his. They all regarded the Lao with a mix of irritation, condescension, and scorn untempered by empathy. Vincent Cillis, top U.S. adviser to the Lao National Police, noted in his 1958 "Terminal Report" that, "The Lao by nature is somewhat indolent, perhaps due to the enervating climate, which reduces mental and physical vigor and produces a 'manana' philosophy." Whatever the reason, he observed, "Most Laotians" were "woefully weak," "strongly indolent," and "unambitious." USOM Deputy Director Gordon Messegee complained in late 1957 that his biggest problem was "the prevailing method of thought, the ideology of the Lao people," which, he said, was "not completely in harmony with that required by a technical civilization." Messegee informed Robert Smither, acting chief of the field service division, that, "While the Laos [sic] tend to let matters take their own course and to seek moderation, an industrial civilization requires people who are ambitious, . . . [who] make a virtue out of precision and exactness, who anticipate the problems of the future, and who have the patience to wait for the benefits in the future derived from investments in the present." As far as Messegee was concerned, those requirements defined the antithesis of the host population. USIS leader Hank Miller's 1958

---

5. Address by historian Sir Michael Howard to the Royal United Services Institute, October 2001, and article, "What's in a Name? How to Fight Terrorism," *Foreign Affairs*, 81 (January–February 2002), pp. 8–13; "hunted down," p. 9.

"Country Plan for Laos" bewailed Lao "Political naïveté" and "unawareness of the responsibilities of good citizenship and good government." There were no "tested, articulate leaders" in the country, he noted, and citizens put no stock in "the value of self-help." Even the team of experts sent to Laos by the International Cooperation Administration (ICA) in early 1958 to evaluate the aid program could not disguise their contempt. While much of their report was accurate and bracingly honest—they condemned the mismanagement of American funds, the "haphazard programming in the field," and the "low level of skill displayed in program execution"—they also described the Lao as "immature," "illiterate," "benighted," "unfamiliar with the twentieth century," and "not vigorous as to health." They were especially dismissive of Lao Buddhism, which, they claimed, "leads to the complacent acceptance of life as it is." "There is certainly no desire on the part of the Lao for economic development," the ICA report averred. "At the very most, they would like more whiskey and more new cars."[6]

This weighty evidentiary paragraph contains twenty-two separate quotations from four different sources, integrated into paraphrased context and interpretive prose. Jacobs, a diplomatic historian in the tradition of the so-called cultural turn of the 1990s, is concerned with policymakers' rhetoric as well as their policies, hence his presentation of individual quoted words in counterpoint to a couple of sentence-length passages. Notice how Jacobs identifies all his speakers, and makes clear whose voice the reader hears, with comments such as, *he observed, they condemned, they claimed.*

Textual Immersion: Michael Chapman, 2009

Underlying Everett's thinking was the premise that it was the "will of Providence, and for the interest of humanity, that America should be settled by a civilized race of men," to which he added an assumption that the "genius" of America's institutions—its unique

---

6. Seth Jacobs, "The Universe Unraveling: United States Policy toward Laos, 1954–62," draft manuscript, January 2010. Jacobs is associate professor of history at Boston College.

government—was the "final design of Providence." Enamored as he was with ancient Greece and Rome, their republics had been short lived, prone to corruption and outside attack; at no time had the ancients been able to capitalize on a "populous and extensive region, blessed with institutions securing enjoyment and transmission of regulated liberty," as Americans now could. An expanding population with access to limitless land was central to Everett's calculus, yet had North America's colonists been European, Providence's final design would have been unfulfilled. "One of the happiest features of the American character" was its "peculiarity" of population, for it was onto the "stock of English civilization" that time had "engrafted the languages, the arts, and the tastes of the other civilized nations." Had Americans been the "unmixed descendents of any one nation of Europe," then—even with perfect governance—they would have retained a "moral and intellectual dependency on that nation," and their experiment would have failed. One of the most "attractive and beautiful peculiarities" of Americans was that they had inherited from the English settlers all the "prominent qualities of the Anglo-Saxon," an "admixture of almost everything that is valuable" in the European states. This was why republicanism had failed in France, where the "former evil" of monarchical tyranny had existed in its most "inveterate form." So despite the "power of example" provided by the United States, the reaction was necessarily violent, with such "dreadful excesses" that the very name of liberty almost became odious. It remained for Americans alone to be "exemplars": they must never forget that because "the eyes of the world" were turned upon them, if they were to fail then they would "blast the hopes of the friends of liberty" throughout the world to eternity.[7]

As the footnote indicates, this paragraph assembles a composite picture of Edward Everett's faith in American exceptionalism, drawn from different passages in a long, Fourth of July oration. I

7. Edward Everett, address at the Charlestown Lyceum, 28 June 1830, Fourth of July Oration in Charlestown, 1828, in *Orations and Speeches . . . by Edward Everett*, pp. 203–4, 143, 151, 157–58, 161, 157.

have interspersed short quotations of rich rhetoric with close paraphrasing in Everett's own style and vocabulary. Far from putting
words into Everett's mouth, because he packed so many passages
of a similar ilk into his delivery, I would argue that I have understated the impact his oration would have had on Bostonians in
1828.

Textual Immersion: Michael Chapman, 2009

Once into the meat of the speech, perhaps warmed by the
brandy and with the wind backing around so his voice carried toward the crowd, Webster's old genius became apparent. Speaking
"slowly and with great deliberation," as one spectator later recalled,
Webster proudly exclaimed, "The Bunker Hill Monument is finished. Here it stands," infinitely high in its objects and purpose,
rising over the land and the sea, visible from the homes of 300,000
citizens of Massachusetts. This was no mere memorial, or work of
art. It had a purpose, a purpose that enrobed it with "dignity and
moral grandeur," a purpose that gave it character. Indeed, the
words they were hearing at that moment came not from mortal
lips but from the very soul of the Monument: it was "the orator of
this occasion." It was a plain shaft. It bore no inscriptions.
"Fronting to the rising sun, from which the future antiquarian
shall wipe the dust," it stood silent. And yet, at the sun's rising and
setting, in the noonday blaze and the "milder effulgence of lunar
light; it looks, it speaks, it acts, to the full comprehension of every
American mind." In its blank anonymity—Webster was explaining—lay the Monument's oracle-like purpose, "Its silent, but awful utterance." On that day, it happened to be speaking to them
through Webster, just as it would speak to them in future oratories
through successive generations of Americans, as they rose up before it, and gathered around it. Because of its special character, its
message, he predicted, would always be "of patriotism and courage; of civil and religious liberty; of free government; of the moral
improvement and elevation of mankind." For theirs was a civilization founded on solid science, informed by knowledge of nature
and the arts, stimulated by moral sentiment, and purified by the

truths of Christianity.[8]

[Original text:] The Bunker Hill Monument is finished. Here it stands. Fortunate in the high natural eminence on which it is placed, higher, infinitely higher in its objects and purpose, it rises over the land and over the sea; and, visible, at their homes, to three hundred thousand of the people of Massachusetts, it stands a memorial of the last, and a monitor to the present, and to all succeeding generations. I have spoken of the loftiness of its purpose. If it had been without any other design than the creation of a work of art, the granite of which it is composed would have slept in its native bed. It has a purpose, and that purpose gives it its character. That purpose enrobes it with dignity and moral grandeur. That well-known purpose it is which causes us to look up to it with a feeling of awe. It is itself the orator of this occasion. It is not from my lips, it could not be from any human lips, that that strain of eloquence is this day to flow most competent to move and excite the vast multitudes around me. The powerful speaker stands motionless before us. It is a plain shaft. It bears no inscriptions, fronting to the rising sun, from which the future antiquarian shall wipe the dust. Nor does the rising sun cause tones of music to issue from its summit. But at the rising of the sun, and at the setting of the sun; in the blaze of noonday, and beneath the milder effulgence of lunar light; it looks, it speaks, it acts, to the full comprehension of every American mind, and the awakening of glowing enthusiasm in every American heart. Its silent, but awful utterance; its deep pathos, as it brings to our contemplation the 17th of June, 1775, and the consequences which have resulted to us, to our country, and to the world, from the events of that day, and which we know must continue to rain influence on the destinies of mankind to the end of time; the elevation with which it raises us high above the ordinary feelings of life,—surpass all that

---

8. George Frisbie Hoar, *Autobiography of Seventy Years* (New York: Charles Scribner's Sons, 1903), I, p. 135; Daniel Webster, *An Address Delivered at the Completion of the Bunker Hill Monument, June 17, 1843* (Boston: Tappan and Dennet, 1843), pp. 5–6.

the study of the closet, or even the inspiration of genius, can produce. To-day it speaks to us. Its future auditories will be the successive generations of men, as they rise up before it and gather around it. Its speech will be of patriotism and courage; of civil and religious liberty; of free government; of the moral improvement and elevation of mankind; and of the immortal memory of those who, with heroic devotion, have sacrificed their lives for their country. . . . But if the civilization of the present race of men, founded, as it is, in solid science, the true knowledge of nature, and vast discoveries in art, and which is elevated and purified by moral sentiment and by the truths of Christianity, be not destined to destruction before the final termination of human existence on earth, the object and purpose of this edifice will be known till that hour shall come.

I have three aims for this paragraph, taken from a draft of a social history of the Bunker Hill Monument, and based on one of Daniel Webster's most inspired orations. First, to recreate the drama and importance of the event; second, to demonstrate Webster's oratorical brilliance and charisma, and third, to explain his notion that the Monument's mute genius was its ability to speak through elites such as himself and Everett. Textual immersion facilitates those aims far better than would complete sentences or a block quotation. Webster's almost excessive opening of sentences with the third-person neuter pronoun *it* lends the passage a directness and an immediacy, which I have tried to mirror in the paraphrasing as well as illustrate in the quotations.

Giving Credit (Not Plagiarizing)

Traumatized as a child by his mother's strict Calvinism, Ickes grew up more like his loose-living father, secular with an ingrained distrust of organized religions, but capped by an "unwavering belief in his own moral rectitude," as one biography puts it.[9]

---

9. For a psychological profile of Ickes's upbringing, see Graham White and John Maze, *Harold Ickes of the New Deal: His Private Life and Public Career* (Cambridge, MA: Harvard University Press, 1985), pp. 12–15, 25.

Biographers Graham White and John Maze show how Ickes, traumatized as a child by his mother's strict Calvinism, grew up more like his loose-living father, secular with an ingrained distrust of organized religions, but capped by an "unwavering belief in his own moral rectitude."[9]

There is a fine line between crediting other scholars and appropriating other scholars' work as your own, a line that is all too easy to cross, often inadvertently. Compare these two sentences, the first from my dissertation, the second from my forthcoming book, which I used to support an argument that Secretary of the Interior Harold Ickes may have been morally predisposed to support the Loyalists in the Spanish Civil War just as he was ill disposed toward America's Catholic hierarchy whose members backed Spain's rival Nationalists. At first sight, both sentences are virtually identical, with a citation to the White and Maze biography. A closer reading indicates otherwise. As I am embarrassed to admit, the first sentence implies that it is either common knowledge or my opinion, presumably based on research I conducted, that Ickes's pious mother traumatized him, his father was a role model, and so forth. But the assertions are neither common knowledge nor the fruits of my research, rather they are the result of the work of White and Maze, as I make explicit in the second version. When I wrote the original sentence, I sought a clear construction that fore-grounded the argument I was making about Ickes's pro-Loyalist activism; it was never my intention to plagiarize, yet I am guilty nonetheless.

Footnotes

10. Justus D. Doenecke, *Storm on the Horizon: The Challenge to American Intervention, 1939–1941* (Lanham, MD: Rowman & Littlefield Publishers, 2003), pp. 170–1.

11. *Congressional Record, House Journal,* 75th Cong., 1st sess., 6 January 1937, p. 99.

12. F. Melder to the editor, *Catholic Worker,* 6:4 (September 1938), p. 5.

13. Doenecke, *Storm on the Horizon,* p. 174.

14. Ibid., p. 180.

15. Dorothea Liebmann Straus, telephone interview by author, 7 October 2005, digital recording and transcription, 25 min., author's collection.

16. Report of confidential informant Harold Neff, 6 May 1943, Federal Bureau of Investigation, file 65-1461, National Archives, College Park, MD, 10:420, emphasis in the original.

17. Charles E. Coughlin, "The Declaration of Independence," Sunday, 10 March 1935, in *A Series of Addresses on Social Justice, as Broadcast by Rev. Charles E. Coughlin Over a National Network, March 1935* (Royal Oak, MI: Radio League of the Little Flower, 1935), pp. 207–18.

18. Radiogram of 18 November, and memorandum from Howe to the mayor of 22 November 1938, in Mayor Fiorello La Guardia Papers, Municipal Archives of New York City, reel 530, documents 1376–80 (hereafter cited as 530:1376–80).

In this series of typical footnotes, notice the short form of the Doenecke book at the second mention, and the substitution of ibid. in the note directly following. Whenever a quotation has emphasis (italics or underlining) in the original text, I always state in the footnote that it does so; this ensures clarity and consistency because sometimes I remove the emphasis. In the rare event that you add emphasis to a quotation you must always mention it in the footnote ("emphasis added" or "emphasis mine"), just as you should state when you have removed emphasis.

Compound Footnotes

There is a corpus of material, especially from the pre-White House years, that casts light on Roosevelt's disposition toward foreign affairs. Historians of Roosevelt's policymaking often refer to his dislike of the Old World. "Roosevelt's opinion of the French," comments Thomas Fleming, "was almost as low—and as hostile—as his opinion of the Germans." Frederick W. Marks observes that he "harbored little admiration or respect for any of the European powers." John Lamberton Harper stresses Roosevelt's aversion to the backwardness and moral turpitude of Europe, a "distancing" from Old World "decadence" that Harper terms "Europhobic-hemispherism." Perhaps because Roosevelt never visited the Iberian Peninsula, historians pass no comment on his cognitive image or "mental map" of decadent Spain, but circumstantial evidence when taken in sum indicates that it was negative.[40]

40. Thomas Fleming, *The New Dealers' War: FDR and the War Within World War II* (New York: Basic Books, 2001), p. 310; Frederick W. Marks III, *Winds Over Sand: The Diplomacy of Franklin Roosevelt* (Athens: University of Georgia Press, 1988), p. 124; John Lamberton Harper, *American Visions of Europe: Franklin D. Roosevelt, George F. Kennan, and Dean G. Acheson* (New York: Cambridge University Press, 1994), pp. 12–18, "distancing," p. 19, "decadence," p. 26, "Europhobic-hemispherism," p. 60. See Alan K. Henrikson, "The Geographical 'Mental Maps' of American Foreign Policy Makers," *International Political Science Review*, 1:3 (October 1980), pp. 495–530.

Many journal and book publishers require compound footnotes, meaning that you will need to combine the notes for each paragraph, separated by a semicolon, into a single footnote at the paragraph's end. In this example, the references for the Fleming and Marks books were straightforward, and I could have simply provided the Harper page references in the form, pp. 19, 26, 60. But I needed to cite the pages in Harper's study that discuss Roosevelt's aversion to backwardness, as well as make clear which quote was on which page, hence the inclusion in the footnote of the words in quotation marks. Because the footnote was already seventy-six words long at that point, and with Henrikson's work on mental mapping falling into a separate, methodological category from the other references, I decided to break into a new sentence.

Sample Bibliography

BIBLIOGRAPHY

Archival Sources and Unpublished Documents

American Legion. National Convention Proceedings. American Legion Library, Indianapolis.

Cárdenas, Juan F. de. Correspondence. *America* Magazine Archive. Lauinger Library Special Collections, Georgetown University, Washington, DC.

Forbes, William Cameron. Papers [WCFP]. Houghton Library, Harvard College, Cambridge, MA.

———. "Journal of W. Cameron Forbes" [WCFP-J]. Series I, 5 vols.; series II, 5 vols. Compiled ca. 1946. Houghton Library, Harvard College, Cambridge, MA.

Harmon, Louise Benedict. Diaries, 1935–39. Private collection of Louise Meière Dunn, Stamford, CT.

Hart, Merwin K. Papers [MKHP]. Knight Library Special Collections, University of Oregon, Eugene.

———. Correspondence. *America* Magazine Archive. Lauinger Library Special Collections, Georgetown University.

Kelly, John Eoghan. Federal Bureau of Investigation, file 65-1461. National Archives, College Park, MD. Sections 1–11, serials 1–495.

La Guardia, Fiorello. Papers. Municipal Archives of New York City, New York.

Meière, Hildreth. Papers [HMP]. Archives of American Art, Smithsonian Institution, New York.

———. "Trip to Russia." New York: ca. September 1936. 39 pp. In HMP.

———. Untitled memoir, "Spain, August 1938," based on spiral-bound notebooks, "Diary—Spain, [August] 1938." New York: ca. October 1938. 199 pp. (186 pp. plus pp. 24a–24m). In HMP.

Moffat, J. Pierrepont. Diary. Houghton Library, Harvard

College, Cambridge, MA.

O'Reilly, Leonora. Papers. Microfilm edition of Papers of the Women's Trade Union League and Its Principal Leaders. Schlesinger Library, Radcliffe College, Cambridge, MA.

Roosevelt, Franklin D. Papers pertaining to family, business, and personal affairs, 1882–1945. Franklin D. Roosevelt Library, Hyde Park.

————. Papers as President, President's Secretary's File, 1933–45 [FDR-SF]. Franklin D. Roosevelt Library.

State Department. General Records, Central Decimal File, 1930–39, Record Group 59 [SD-CDF]. National Archives, College Park, MD.

Winchell, Walter. Federal Bureau of Investigation, file 62-31615. Available online, at http://foia.fbi.gov/foiaindex/winchell.htm.

Published Documents

American Direct Investments in Foreign Countries–1936. Paul D. Dickens, ed. U.S. Department of Commerce, Bureau of Foreign and Domestic Commerce. Washington, DC: U.S. Government Printing Office (GPO), 1938.

*Atheistic Communism (*Divini Redemptoris*): Encyclical Letter of His Holiness Pope Pius XI.* New York: Paulist Press, 1937.

Confidential U.S. State Department Central Files: Spain; Foreign Affairs & Political, 1930–1939. Bethesda, MD: University Publications of America. Microfilm.

Congressional Record: Proceedings and Debates of the Third Session of the Seventy-fifth Congress of the United States of America. Vol. 83, pt. 6. Washington, DC: U.S. GPO, 1938.

Documents diplomatiques français, 1932–1939 [Diplomatic Documents of France, 1932–1939]. Series 2 (1936–39), 19 vols. Paris: Imprimerie nationale, 1974.

Documents on American Foreign Relations, January 1938–June 1939. S. Shepard Jones and Denys P. Myers, eds. Boston: World Peace Foundation, 1939.

FDR's Fireside Chats. Russell D. Buhite and David W. Levy, eds. Norman: University of Oklahoma Press, 1992.

Franklin D. Roosevelt and Foreign Affairs [FDR-FA]. Edgar B. Nixon, ed. First series. Vols. I–III. Cambridge, MA: Belknap Press, 1969.

Gallup, George H. *The Gallup Poll: Public Opinion, 1935–1971.* New York: Random House, 1972.

Germany and the Spanish Civil War, 1936–1939. Vol. 3 of *Documents on German Foreign Policy, 1918–1945: From the Archives of the German Foreign Ministry: Series D (1937–1945).* Washington, DC: U.S. GPO, 1950.

Investigation of Un-American Activities and Propaganda Activities in the United States: Report of the Special Committee on Un-American Activities. 4 vols., I, II. Washington, DC: U.S. GPO, 1938–39.

The Papers of Thomas Jefferson. Barbara B. Oberg, ed. Vol. 32. Princeton: Princeton University Press, 2005.

Proceedings of the 20th National Convention of The American Legion, Los Angeles, CA, 19–22 September 1938. 76th Cong., 1st sess., House Document no. 40, 53.

Public Papers and Addresses of Franklin D. Roosevelt: With a Special Introduction and Explanatory Notes by President Roosevelt. 1938 Volume: The Continuing Struggle for Liberalism. New York: The Macmillan Company, 1941.

United States Foreign Policy (supplement). *The Reference Shelf,* 13:6. New York: The H.W. Wilson Company, 1939.

Daily Newspapers
Periodicals are for the period of this study, unless otherwise stated.

Chicago Daily Tribune.

Jersey Journal (Jersey City, NJ). 1937–38.

New York Times [*NYT*].

Philadelphia Inquirer. 1938–39.

PM (New York). Ralph Ingersoll, ed. June 1940–43.

Weekly Newspapers and Magazines

America: The National Catholic Weekly. Francis X. Talbot, SJ, ed.

Brooklyn Tablet (Brooklyn, NY). Patrick F. Scanlan, ed. Published every Saturday by the Tablet Publishing Company.

The Hour (New York). American Council Against Nazi Propaganda. Albert E. Kahn, ed. 30 April 1939–20 May 1943.

Ken (Chicago). Arnold Gingrich, ed. Biweekly. April 1938– March 1939.

New Masses (New York). Max Eastman, ed. 1936–37.

News of Spain (New York). Spanish Information Bureau. Biweekly. February 1938–February 1939.

Time: The Weekly Newsmagazine. November 1936–39.

Weekly Foreign Letter (New York). Lawrence Dennis, ed. June 1938–July 1942.

Monthly Magazines and Journals

Catholic Action: A National Monthly (Washington, DC). National Catholic Welfare Conference.

Protestant Digest (New York). K. Leslie, ed. Monthly to May 1940, then bimonthly. December 1938–September 1941.

The Sign (Union City, NJ). "A National Catholic Magazine." Rev. Theophane Maquire, ed. 1936–41.

Spain: A Monthly Publication of Spanish Events (New York). Joseph M. Bayo, ed. Peninsular News Service. October 1937–January 1942.

Films

Blockade. Directed by William Dieterle. Starring: Madeleine Carroll and Henry Fonda. Producer: Walter Wanger. Script: John Howard Lawson. United Artists, 1938. DVD, 84 min. Chatsworth, CA: Image Entertainment, 1987.

"My Tour of Nationalist Spain, August 1938, by Hildreth Meière." Hildreth Meière. 16mm, 3 reels, Archives of

American Art, Smithsonian Institution, New York. DVD,
33 min., author's collection.

Interviews

Dunn, Louise Meière. Interview by author, 29 October 2005.
Stamford, CT. Digital recording and transcription, 120
min., author's collection.

Sedgwick, Ellery, Jr. Telephone interview by author, 10 May
2004. Longwood University, Farmville, VA.

Memoirs, Diaries, Contemporary Works

Acheson, Dean G. *Present at the Creation: My Years in the State
Department.* New York: W.W. Norton & Company,
1969.

[Adams, John.] *Diary and Autobiography of John Adams.* L.H.
Butterfield, ed. Vol. II. Cambridge: Belknap Press, 1962.

Browder, Earl. "The American Communist Party in the
Thirties." In *As We Saw the Thirties: Essays on Social and
Political Movements of a Decade.* Rita James Simon, ed.
Urbana: University of Illinois Press, 1967.

Carlson, John Roy [(Arthur) Avedis Derounian]. *Under Cover:
My Four Years in the Nazi Underworld of America—The
Amazing Revelation of How Axis Agents and Our Enemies
Within Are Now Plotting to Destroy the United States.* New
York: E.P. Dutton & Company, 1943.

———. *The Plotters.* New York: E.P. Dutton & Company,
1946.

Dalton, Joseph Patrick. "Is Christian Corporatism Compatible
with Democracy?" Master's thesis, Boston College,
Chestnut Hill, MA, 1942.

Eberle, George T. "Portugal's Progress." WNAC radio address,
29 May 1938. *Catholic Mind,* 36:854 (22 July 1938), pp.
282–87.

Gomá y Tomás, Cardinal Isidro. *Por Dios y por España:
Pastorales–Instrucciones pastorales y Artículos–Discursos–
Mensajes–Apéndice, 1936–1939* [For God and for Spain:

Collected Pastoral Letters, Articles, Sermons, and Radio Addresses, 1936–1939]. Barcelona: R. Casulleras, Librero-Editor, 1940.

González Palencia, Angel. *The Flame of Hispanicism.* Lecture given at Stanford University, July 1938. New York: Peninsular News Service, 1938. Pamphlet, 14 pp.

Hart, Merwin Kimball. "America—Look at Spain: The Agony will be Repeated Here." Speech; broadcast from Málaga, 29 September 1938. Printed in *Spain*, 3:1 (15 October 1938), 5, 7, 20, and in *Vital Speeches of the Day*, 5:2 (1 November 1938), pp. 57–58.

Ickes, Harold L. *The Inside Struggle, 1936–1939.* Vol. 2 of *The Secret Diary of Harold L. Ickes.* New York: Simon and Schuster, 1954.

[Johnson, Hiram.] *The Diary Letters of Hiram Johnson, 1917–1945.* Robert E. Burke, ed. 7 vols. New York: Garland Publishing, 1983.

A Little Book for Immigrants in Boston. Boston: Committee for Americanism of the City of Boston, 1921.

St.-George, Maximilian J., and Lawrence Dennis. *A Trial on Trial: The Great Sedition Trial of 1944.* N.p: National Civil Rights Committee, 1945.

Writers Take Sides: Letters About the War in Spain, from 418 American Authors. New York: League of American Writers, 1938.

Published Works, Journal Articles, and Dissertations

ABC Blue Book, Publisher's Statements: Newspapers. Chicago: The Bureau, 1945.

Alpers, Benjamin L. *Dictators, Democracy, and American Public Culture: Envisioning the Totalitarian Enemy, 1920s–1950s.* Chapel Hill: University of North Carolina Press, 2003.

American Law Reports: Federal, Cases and Annotations. Vol. 67. Rochester, NY: Lawyers Co-Operative Publishing Co., 1984, pp. 774–96.

Balfour, Sebastian. "Spain from 1931 to the Present." In *Spain: A History*. Raymond Carr, ed. Oxford: Oxford University Press, 2000.

Brooks, Frank. "Egoist Theory and America's Individualist Anarchists: A Dilemma of Praxis." *History of Political Thought*, 15:3 (Autumn 1994), pp. 403–22.

Costello, Brian C. "The Voice of Government as an Abridgement of First Amendment Rights of Speakers: Rethinking *Meese v. Keene*." *Duke Law Journal* (1989), pp. 654–58.

Costigliola, Frank. "Broken Circle: The Isolation of Franklin D. Roosevelt in World War II." *Diplomatic History*, 32:5 (November 2008), pp. 677–718.

Davis, Richard Akin. "Radio Priest: The Public Career of Father Charles Edward Coughlin." PhD diss., University of North Carolina, Chapel Hill, 1974.

Hobsbawm, Eric J. *Nations and Nationalism Since 1780: Programme, Myth, Reality*. Cambridge: Cambridge University Press, 1990.

———. *The Age of Extremes: A History of the World, 1914–1991*. New York: Vintage Books, 1994.

Lojendio, Luis María de. *Operaciones militares de la guerra de España, 1936–1939* [Military Operations During the Spanish Civil War, 1936–1939]. Barcelona: Montaner y Simon, 1940.

Martin, John. "In the Beginnings of 'Pacific Service': Early Stages of Hydro-Electric Development in North-Central California." *Pacific Service Magazine*, part I, 13:7 (December 1921), pp. 205–15, part II, 13:8 (January 1922), pp. 244–50.

McCarthy, Edward C. "The Christian Front Movement in New York City, 1938–1940." Master's thesis, Columbia University, 1965.

Moynihan, Daniel Patrick. *"Catholic Tradition and Social Change," Second Annual Seton-Neumann Lecture, May*

7, 1984, Rayburn House. N.p.: United States Catholic Conference, 1984.

Payne, Stanley G. *Fascism in Spain, 1923–1977.* Madison: University of Wisconsin Press, 1999.

————. *The Spanish Civil War, The Soviet Union, and Communism.* New Haven: Yale University Press, 2004.

Sandeen, Eric J. "*Confessions of a Nazi Spy* and the German-American Bund." *American Studies,* 20:2 (Fall 1979), pp. 69–81.

Singleton, M.K. *H.L. Mencken and the* American Mercury *Adventure.* Durham, NC: Duke University Press, 1962.

Sterne, Evelyn Savidge. "Beyond the Boss: Immigration and American Political Culture from 1880 to 1940." In *E Pluribus Unum? Contemporary and Historical Perspectives on Immigrant Political Incorporation.* Gary Gerstle and John Mollenkopf, eds. New York: Russell Sage Foundation, 2001.

Wang Hongbin 王鴻賓, ed. *Zhang Zuolin he Fengxi junfa* 張作霖和奉系軍閥 [Zhang Zuolin and the Fengtian Warlords]. N.p.: Hunan renmin chibanshe, 1989.

Zhao Xijun. "'Bu zhan er quren zhi bing' yu xiandai weishe zhanlue" ["Victory without war" and modern deterrence strategy]. *Zhongguo Junshi Kexue* [Chinese Military Science], 5 (2001).

————

Subheads will vary according to the project, although there will usually be three main groupings for unpublished and published primary sources, and secondary sources. List two or more works by the same author in ascending order of publication. Set translations of titles inside square brackets and use roman; this is because italicization specifies the actual, text-searchable title of the publication (a given translation may not even be literal); as the last examples show, there are two styles, with or without the original characters. I prefer abbreviated postal acronyms for states; there is no need to give states when the state is part of the publisher's name (University of North Carolina Press).

DOING HISTORY

While most of the issues stressed in this guide are applicable to any discipline, history does have specific considerations. History is about change over time, and is often concerned with pivotal events and turning points. Although data has its uses, history is primarily involved with the interpretation of textual sources. History is a broad discipline—broader even than geographers considered their vast subject three decades ago—including the history of paintings, music, ideas, diseases, and warships, yet it should ultimately be a study of people and what makes them so fallibly human. Unlike the mathematical and physical sciences, when it comes to *doing history* there is rarely, if ever, only one correct answer, which raises the issue of empiricism or objectivity, and hence argumentation, that I would like to address here in a concluding remark.

When I assign my Chinese students their first analytical essay based on primary source material, with part of the grade dependent on the strength and originality of the argument, there are objections. "We have come to this university to learn how to be good historians," they say, "so providing we study the evidence correctly, we must all reach the same conclusion. Only those who make a different argument deserve a bad grade." It is hard to refute this logic, which reminds me of my father's recommendation to read Winston Churchill's history of World War II: "I'm sure you'll agree it's a thoroughly good job because Churchill presents the facts." Yet my Chinese students would no doubt disagree with the historical facts Churchill presented to support his argument for the civilizing benefits of British imperialism. Academic historians, for sure, should strive for objectivity, but not even in the state archives of Shangri-la did primary source texts embody empirical truth.

A nation-state's official history reaches its citizens in large part through their primary school education, becoming received wisdom that reinforces the cycle when citizen historians write new textbooks. Citizens and officials alike have such vested interests in establishing a national consensus that any challenge to the facts of, say, a patriotic war can be tantamount to treason. It is unsurprising, therefore, that one nation's wartime history, along with all the historiography necessary to support the edifice, sounds so different from another nation's. A given history, I therefore suggest, is only as true as those reading it judge it to be, which is why good historians are those who write convincing theses, who *advance a proposition as an argument*. Good luck with your thesis, only I hope that after reading this guide you do not need it.

GLOSSARY

block quotation (extract) a lengthy quoted passage of 100 words or more, indented, as a paragraph, without quotation marks, and typically set in a smaller font size.

body paragraph situated between introductory and concluding paragraphs, of around 250–350 words, beginning with a topic sentence and ending with a concluding remark, transitioning into the following paragraph, being of an evidentiary or interpretive nature, and typically containing or advancing a single main point that is a component part of the thesis.

citation your formal acknowledgment of the source—primary or secondary—for a specific quotation, idea, argument, body of information, or factual data (other than common knowledge) that you have employed in your work, consisting of a footnote reference number and an accompanying footnote containing information that accurately references the source. First, it tells your reader that the information you are presenting derives not from your original thinking or first-hand observation but rather from another source; second, it enables the reader to visit the source in order to verify that the information you have provided is correct.

cliometrics a historiographical method that relies on data, computational modeling, and/or statistics, typically in the fields of economic or environmental history. An archetype was *Time on the Cross* by economists Robert Fogel and Stanley Engerman, which argued that plantation slavery was less profitable than free labor would otherwise have been.

dissertation a doctoral dissertation, typically adjudicated by a committee (advisor and two to four readers), presented at a public defense, comprising a scholarly, multi-chapter monograph based on archival research, of around 300–500 double-spaced pages (80,000–140,000 words), and which presents an original and significant thesis.

field   a major branch of your discipline; early-modern Chinese, French diplomatic, global environmental, U.S. labor, and ancient military history are all fields of the discipline of history.

finding aid   a device—from a card index to an online text-searchable database—that enables a researcher to evaluate the contents of an archival collection.

footnote reference   a note, set at the bottom of the page in 10-point type, identifying a source with sufficient accuracy for another researcher to easily locate it.

footnote reference number   a superscripted Arabic numeral placed at the end of a sentence (or paragraph for a compound footnote) that identifies a matching footnote reference located at the bottom of the page.

journal article   a research paper generally of 6,500 words intended for a peer-reviewed scholarly publication.

master's thesis   similar to a doctoral dissertation but typically of shorter length, with less emphasis on the originality and significance of the thesis (argument), and not always subject to a public defense.

précis   cut the clutter—vanquish the verbiage; French (render with precision), in common usage in British English, meaning to shorten, to present the gist of a passage by discarding unnecessary detail.

primary source   an original source such as a diary, memoir, letter, report, speech, newspaper article, interview, photograph, cartoon, film, or artifact created at the time of, or directly pertaining to, the period under study.

road map   a description, overview, or list that maps out the structure—the main points in the order they appear—of your paper, chapter, or entire project, typically located at the end of an introductory paragraph or section.

secondary source   a work such as a journal article or monograph that relies on original primary sources, or a synthesis that draws in large measure on other secondary sources that are themselves based on primary sources; in the case of a historiographical study or contemporary critique, secondary sources can become primary sources.

senior research paper (senior honors thesis, school year thesis, graduation thesis)   similar to a master's thesis but conducted at the undergraduate level to less exacting standards.

subhead   a heading set in distinctive bold or italicized type, at the start of a section or main-point break in an article or chapter, typically of between one and two thousand words.

thesis   *a proposition advanced as an argument*; in its concrete form, a scholarly work of archival research that makes an original argument, such as a research paper, MA thesis, or doctoral dissertation.

topic   a subset of your field that frames the subject of your research.

topic sentence   introduces a paragraph and suggests or describes its function in the context of your thesis; a paragraph without a topic sentence will lack purpose and direction.